RELENTLESS
Mark Victor Hansen

Wisdom Behind the Incomparable
Chicken Soup for the Soul

MITZI PERDUE

Copyright © 2022 by Mitzi Perdue
Relentless: Mark Victor Hansen
Wisdom Behind the Incomparable Chicken Soup for the Soul
All rights reserved. No part of this publication may be reproduced, distributed, or transmitted in any form or by any means, including photocopying, recording, or other electronic or mechanical methods, without the prior written permission of the publisher, except in the case of brief quotations embodied in critical reviews and certain other noncommercial uses permitted by copyright law.
For permission requests, write to the publisher, addressed "Attention: Permissions Coordinator," carol@markvictorhansenlibrary.com

Quantity sales special discounts are available on quantity purchases by corporations, associations, and others. For details, contact the publisher at carol@markvictorhansenlibrary.com

Orders by U.S. trade bookstores and wholesalers.
Email: carol@markvictorhansenlibrary.com

Cover Design - Low & Joe Creative, Brea, CA 92821
Book Layout - DBree - StoneBear Design

Manufactured and printed in the United States of America distributed globally by markvictorhansenlibrary.com

New York | Los Angeles | London | Sydney

ISBN: 979-8-88581-042-5 Hardcover
ISBN: 979-8-88581-043-2 Paperback
ISBN: 979-8-88581-044-9 eBook

Library of Congress Control Number: 2022910723

CONTENTS

Dedication 6

Acknowledgements 7

Introduction 9

1. Mark's Childhood. 12
2. Teen Years and How Mark Became Beatles 2.0. 27
3. Mark's College Experience: Academics, and a Summer in India. 41
4. Graduate School and Buckminster Fuller. 52
5. Bankruptcy and Finding His Purpose. 57
6. The Ultimate Mentor, Rev. Ike 67
7. Mark in His Thirties 73
8. Mark Changes a High School Graduate's Life 76
9. Bob Proctor, Business Partner, Mastermind Partner, and Lifelong Friend 82
10. How Soup Got Started 89
11. Selling Soup: A Case Study in Perseverance 95
12. Selling Chicken Soup: The Ultimate Don't Quit Story. . .100
13. Selling Chicken Soup to the Public 108
14. Chicken Soup Sales Make History. 118
15. Mark in His Fifties: Scaling the Pinnacles of His Professional Life. 126
16. A Major Failure: Mark's First Marriage 137

17. Choosing a Spouse the Second Time 147
18. Relationship with Stepchildren, and Daughters 161
19. Helping Friends, Mark Continues to Touch Lives 169
20. His Sixties: What Does a Man Like Mark
    Do for an Encore?. 182
21. A Fifty-Year-Old Friendship, the Lehrers. 188
22. Tithing, a Bedrock Principle that Guides Mark's Life . . .193
23. Mark and Childhelp 197
24. Mark and Teaching Others to Give 203
25. Mark and the Nation's Blood Supply 208
26. Other Friends Talk about Mark 216
27. Ken Walls, Proof of the Power of Stories 221
28. The Power of Stories, and How They Can
    Change Your Life 224
29. The Next Chapter 231
30. Conclusion. 234
    Epilogue 236
    In Closing 238
    About Mitzi Perdue. 248

RELENTLESS | 5

Dedication

If you have been victimized by human trafficking,
If you are working to combat this scourge,

If you are a member of the UBS Optimus Foundation who's working to eliminate trafficking in Bangladesh in order to learn how to eliminate it everywhere,

This book is dedicated to you!

Mitzi Perdue, Author, Speaker, Anti-trafficking Advocate
www.MitziPerdue.com
+1 410 860 4444 (NYC Time)

Acknowledgements

The Crazy Rat Club was my true emotional support team. What? You don't know who the Crazy Rats are?

They're my older sister, Augusta Petrone, and older brother, Barclay Henderson. Once a week during a Zoom call, they'd encourage me during my writing of Relentless. The three of us have been encouraging each other for close to eighty years. When we were four, six, and eight years old, we decided we loved each other and were fun to be with. That's never changed. To me, one of life's greatest blessings is having fun and supportive siblings who encourage you. Thanks, Rats, for encouraging me when I was writing *Relentless*!

However, the Rats aren't the only ones I'm grateful to. Cindy Downes, who's worked in my office for 30 years, is the fabulous person who keeps Ship Mitzi afloat. She's the professional's professional and is usually five steps ahead of me on What Practical Things Need to Be Done Right Now. Cindy, thank you for helping keep Relentless on track.

Carol McManus and Dana Bree are the genius ladies who took charge of all the details for editing, designing, and publishing Relentless. For awhile, I took to calling myself, "the McManus Migraine," because I'd interrupt Carol and Dana as well with oddball requests such as, "I think the ISBN numbers are wrong!" (They weren't) Anyway, I'm endlessly grateful for their patience and professionalism.

I'd also like to thank Preston Weekes, who's Mark's stepson and Crystal's son. I had endless IT questions for Preston,

Acknowledgements

but he was unfailingly kind and patient with whatever was baffling me.

The biggest shout-out is to the 66 individuals who were willing to share their memories and insights about Mark. Many (and probably most) biographers have to research historical documents for their materials. I got to do my research courtesy of "living libraries," that is, people who draw on their own memories and experience. For me it was sheer joy, having the chance to peer into their worlds and learn about Mark through their eyes.

I said the biggest shout-out was to the 66 individuals who talked with me about Mark. One of these was Mark himself. For me, one of the most fascinating parts of creating this book is that even though there were people who spoke negatively about Mark, when I showed him the final text, he didn't ask me to change a single comma. He was totally on board with a "warts and all" portrait of himself. He wanted honesty. I admire him for that.

To all of you, my deepest gratitude.

Introduction
Who is Mark Victor Hansen?

There's a good chance you know about Mark from the Chicken Soup for the Soul series. These books have sold more than half a billion copies. Or maybe you've heard his lectures, or participated in his conferences, or watched him on YouTube.

Mark Victor Hansen's public persona is well known, but what is he like when he's out of the public eye? Who is the person behind the curtain, the person who struggles, hurts, and deals with discouragement and rejection? What are his successes and failures? What makes him tick?

Is he a real-life Harold Hill from *The Music Man*, a flimflam man who's exceptionally good at promoting? Or is he St. Mark, a spiritual man who exists to serve others and wants nothing more than to share his knowledge to promote your growth and enlightenment?

We'll be looking at the good, the bad, and the ugly. We'll examine the opinions of people whose lives he's changed for the better and who are certain that he deserves the title "St. Mark." We'll also examine cases where people see him as mostly a promoter, a man who's gone through a bankruptcy, a failed marriage, a fraught relationship with the original publisher of *Chicken Soup for the Soul*, and changes that ended a once-vibrant partnership with his co-author.

His successes are well-known but what about his failures? What can we learn together from both his large collection of successes and his impressive set of failures?

RELENTLESS | 9

Introduction

This brings me to a second part of what this book is about. Besides discovering who Mark Victor Hansen is, you'll also discover tips to help you develop your own success story. You'll learn about what it takes to sell half a billion books, be on The New York Times Best Seller list with fifty-seven different books, and make as much as $225,000 for a package of three speeches. And you'll be inspired by some of his favorite quotes; words that resonate with people in every corner of the globe.

I guarantee you that Mark's successes didn't just drop in his lap. You'll get to see how he accomplished what he did, what he learned from his failures, and how these failures propelled him to further success. Most important, you can use Mark's principles to build the future of your dreams.

The principles you'll read in this book work. And you don't need to have unusual gifts to make them work for you. Each one of the principles is something you can do starting today. If you build even one of them into your life, you'll be ahead of the game. Do several of them, and you'll be surprised by how far they'll take you. Do most of them, and you'll get further than you ever dreamed.

What about doing all of them? If you can do all of them, well, you must be Mark Victor Hansen himself.

Ah, something else before we start: Here's a little about me, your guide on this journey and some hints about what else you'll find in this book. As with all biographers, I have a particular lens through which I view my subject. My lens is that people who have enormous impact fascinate me. I saw how my late father co-founded and guided the company as president of the Sheraton Hotel chain. My late husband Frank Perdue grew his father-and-son chicken operation into a company that today employs 21,000 people and is the largest producer of organic chicken in the world. As you continue reading, I'll mention how some of Mark's success principles also worked for building this giant hotel chain and a global poultry business.

Although I've written twenty-seven books, this one is different. This book will not follow the usual format for biographies. I'm writing this book for you. I'm going to be addressing you, telling you what I think about things, even urging you to do something. That's probably a first in a biography. The chapter on something remarkable Mark Victor Hansen did for the American Red Cross Blood Bank holds a surprise for you. By the time we get there, you won't find it shocking. Maybe you'll even find it's something that people from across the political spectrum can embrace and act on.

My hope for this book is that you'll find it inspirational. That means I'm not going to wallow in negativity. I'll mention negative things for learning purposes, but they're not the focus of this book. I believe that the "Law of Attraction" is true, that you attract what you focus on.

Come along for the ride! Along the way, enjoy insights that may help you further along the road to being who you want to be.

– Mitzi Perdue

1 Mark's Childhood

When Mark Victor Hansen talks about his childhood, it's a little like a Rorschach test, the psychological test where you describe what you see in an inkblot and, in the process, reveal insights about yourself.

Mark's early childhood memories are almost uniformly happy, fun, and adventurous, or about getting away with things. Since we become the stories we tell ourselves, we have a clue right from the beginning about what makes Mark tick. As Mark Willie, one of his friends from later in life says, "Mark is off-the-chart on the optimism scale."

Most people remember an abundance of good, bad, and terrible events from their childhoods, but no matter how long you press Mark for various childhood memories, he invariably frames them as upbeat and a cause for laughter.

Mark's childhood wasn't completely wonderful as we'll see later in this book. But, as in the Rorschach test, it's how he frames it. Deliberately or not, the story he tells himself is one of gratitude, fun, adventure, a bit of self-mockery, and most of all, a strong sense of family.

He starts out with something strikingly affirmative. "I used to overhear my mother tell the patrons at Dad's bakery, as well as Mabel at the grocery store, 'I have the best boys on the block.'" Then adds in passing, "We all did our best to live up to her claim."

1. Mark's Childhood

He goes on to report, "Mom's nightly prayers with each of us from birth ended with the line, 'May Bay, Eric, Mark, and Brian be happy and healthy.'"

When talking about his childhood, Mark's relationship with money is also one of the things he mentions early in the discussion. Unlike some of the kids from other nearby families, he and his siblings weren't given an allowance. His father instilled in them before they were teens they needed to work to buy the things they wanted. Mark was willing to work hard to earn the things he wanted. From a young age, he was focused on creating abundance.

There's a saying here that applies to Mark and his brothers. "Adversity breeds character. Prosperity breeds monsters." Not having an allowance wasn't exactly adversity, but it did a lot to breed character in the young Hansen boys.

Mark once shared, "My three siblings and I were enthusiastic workers. We had to figure out our own ways to earn spending money which meant a lot of lawn mowing, window washing, snow shoveling, even greeting card sales. It was good early training because all of us went on to have successful, lucrative business careers."

Brother Brian, exactly two years and three days younger than Mark, shared a bedroom and countless childhood adventures. As Mark looks at it, "Our proximity in age had great benefits for me. When we were little, we did everything together. We played, worked, lived, and moved in unison. I learned and practiced my leadership, promotion, and sales skills on him."

Brian also has warm memories of this period in their lives. "We shared a bedroom through most of the 1950s, and we did pretty much everything together. While we're

1. Mark's Childhood

both Capricorns, he was extroverted and I was introverted. I remember he was always interested in anything new and different."

Mark's interest in the "new and different" could get both boys in trouble. As Mark puckishly points out, when they did get in trouble, he was usually the instigator. And it fell on his mother to be the disciplinarian in the family.

"In her attempt to master and keep running a home filled with the testosterone of four hyperactive sons and our Dad, she was the one who had to spank us," he remembers. "It was rare but occasional. We deserved it, I'm sure. She never hurt us, but she wanted to make us aware of our digression from her rules—like the simplicity of safely crossing a street by looking first to the left and then to the right. She repeatedly told us to mind her or suffer the consequences—a spanking or a time out."

Mark was responsible for getting Brian and himself in trouble when he was still four and Brian was two. "It came from my early desire to see the world, travel extensively, and experience everything firsthand. This is a lust that has never wavered."

His parents had a rule that the kids were always to stay in their ultra-safe neighborhood where they knew all their neighbors by sight. "I was almost five when I grabbed my little brother's hand, and off we went to explore the world. Amazingly, we walked two miles downtown to my father's Elite Bakery."

The problem was, as Mark explained it, "We had not announced that we were off to see the world. We thought we were simply acting on the affirmation our mother used to repeat, 'I have things to do, places to go, people to meet.'"

Disappearing without telling anyone was not what Mrs. Hansen had in mind with that particular affirmation. Mark remembers, "While we were missing, our mother panicked. First, she was curious, then furious, and then white-hot mad. She looked everywhere she thought we could be. She never imagined we'd be two miles away."

She called all the neighbors, assuming the boys must have gone to someone's home without notifying her. None of them had any idea where the boys might be.

"She feared we'd been kidnapped," Mark reports, adding wryly, "although she couldn't figure out who'd want us."

After she endured more than an hour of sheer terror, she got the phone call from Mark's dad. The four-year-old listened as his father spoke into the handset of the bakery's old rotary-dial telephone, "The boys are here. Yes, I mean at the bakery! No, I don't know how they did it. Marky said they walked here."

To this day, Mark is sure that his dad, being a man who loved to explore, travel, and go on adventures, was secretly proud of what his two little boys did that day. Mark also is pretty sure his dad would never admit this to his rightfully furious wife.

Mark's dad escorted them to the car and drove the two miscreants home. Mark remembers, "Mom moved through our home with speed, grace, and agility. She wore flat slippers that she called 'duffers.' They slapped the back of her heels when she walked, so we knew her whereabouts. We heard her coming!"

They were no sooner out of their father's car than their mother promptly administered a spanking with one of the

1. Mark's Childhood

duffers. Then she put the youngsters in separate corners of the dining room where the two, as if on cue, began to bawl.

As Mark tells it, "As soon as Mom walked out of the room, we started laughing and couldn't stop—deep belly laughs. We had explored the world and returned safely—our first stellar self-generated achievement—without any serious repercussions."

They stopped laughing and turned the tears back on moments later when their mother re-entered the room. They managed, figuratively speaking, to produce buckets of tears. Soon their mother's anger subsided, and Mark noticed that she was having a hard time holding back a smile. Mark could tell she was more relieved than angry, and happy that her two boys were back safe.

"Okay then, have you learned your lesson to obey me?" she asked.

In unison Mark said they chorused, "Yes."

"You are released again, but stay near home in the neighborhood, and come when I call you to dinner. Do you both hear me?"

"Yes, Mommy," we replied meekly.

They had plenty of adventures after that, and it wasn't the last time they were in trouble. One of those wasn't Mark's fault.

Eric Hansen is four years older than Mark, and it was probably he who tested the limits of the Hansen parents the most.

"Eric made life unusual and exciting," says Mark. "I remember one time, Dad brought us up to the Wisconsin-Illinois state line where it was legal to buy fireworks. Eric, Brian, and I had our own money to buy pretty much whatever we wanted—sparklers, exploding caps, firecrackers, pyrotechnics. Even class B special fireworks from China. We each loaded up on them."

Eric happened to be particularly fond of cherry bombs. In case you're younger than sixty, you probably aren't familiar with cherry bombs. Most people today don't know about a true 1950s cherry bomb because they were banned under the federal Child Protection Act of 1966. The true cherry bomb was both impressively loud, and fairly dangerous. It was the size, and color of a real cherry, and the inch-and-a-half long fuse was green to mimic the color of a cherry stem.

By the early 1960s, and before they were banned, the cherry bombs explosive load had been reduced to only 5 percent of the amount of explosive of the cherry bombs Eric Hansen was playing with. In other words, the cherry bombs he purchased on that trip were more like actual small bombs than toys.

Eric got to wondering whether his cherry bomb would explode underwater. He couldn't resist the challenge of testing them with an audience of his best buddies and brothers, Brian and Mark.

There was a problem.

Their mother had just received a birthday present from their father, a beautifully detailed birdbath that instantly became one of her most prized possessions. She cherished it. She loved watching all the birds fly into the backyard and dance around, playing, preening, and cleaning themselves in her four-inch-deep birdbath. Mark sometimes watched her, enjoying the frolicking birds, and he knew the birdbath was her pride and joy.

1. Mark's Childhood

That pretty scene was about to end forever. It was dusk on the third of July 1954. Eric gathered his little brothers around to share the excitement as he lit the fuse, and then threw the cherry bomb with it's burning fuse into the birdbath. Seconds from the time Eric lit the fuse, the bomb exploded. The water in the birdbath erupted in an upward fountain. It was a sight to behold! The boys were entranced . . . for about another second.

Roughly one second later the mini-bomb blasted the birdbath into thousands of pieces.

Mark remembers that it felt like a "head for the hills" moment, but there were no hills to head for. The boys were all screaming. Their parents rushed out of the house, terrified that someone was badly hurt.

The birdbath lay in ruins. "Our parents were temporarily speechless, and then we heard mom shout, 'Eric, get in the house this minute and don't come out until we say so. The party is over!'"

That permanently ended the childhood trips to the state line to buy 4th of July fireworks.

Mark's oldest brother Bay was a strong, fit, bodybuilder. He got Mark interested in fitness and health. He was also a hunter with both a gun and a bow and arrow.

"He took me to the archery range, and I actually got good at target practice," Mark remembers. "We also went carp fishing together. Fishing in a fast-moving river is interesting because, unless the fish are near the surface, the gushing water distorts the image of exactly where you are. I broke many arrows learning that lesson."

For Mark it was exciting to bring home fish for his mother to cook, especially to do it with his big brother who had taught him how. His mother asked, "Why don't you boys shoot real tasty fish?"

Bay smiled and said, "We can only shoot what's in the Des Plaines River, Mom. Carp it is." It was one of many things Mark learned from his older brother.

Mark's first serious, salaried job was at nine years of age, as a paperboy delivering the *Chicago Tribune and Sun Times*. It was frequently below zero, in Waukegan, Illinois, and sometimes as low as twenty below zero. Mark has the tenderest memories of brother Bay back then. Bay was eleven years older, and Mark had always looked up to him.

"Bay saw my flimsy gloves weren't warm enough, so he gave me an expensive pair of giant mittens–deep, ultra-cold weather mittens he had gotten from working at the Edison Company. They prevented my youthful hands from freezing and breaking from the cold. I offered to pay for them, but typical of his gentle and thoughtful kindness, he would accept nothing."

For Mark, his brother Bay was a mentor in many ways. "I looked up to Bay. He was my earliest, and easiest up-close-and-personal role model. He was good looking—even handsome—and suave, occasionally elegant. I watched the tantalizing excitement of him going to two proms during his junior and senior high school years.

"Dressed to the nines in a tuxedo, he was poised, calm, with the demeanor of the actor Clint Eastwood. He was also the cool, strong, silent type who just confidently knew that he knew.

"He had a photographic memory, great painting and sculpting abilities, and on top of that, he owned a brand-new, blue-on-white Chevy Bel Air car, a hog Harley motorcycle,

1. Mark's Childhood

had a lovely girlfriend, a high paying job that put money in his pocket, and lots of friends who loved him and hung out with him at our home."

As Mark puts it, Bay was also brilliant when it came to mechanical things. "He knew all the secrets of machinery, mechanics, electronics, and he could fix anything. The top of his hands had perpetual scratch marks from working on the innards of car engines."

Mark says, "To this day, when I scratch myself, and draw blood, I can see in my mind's eye Bay doing the same, licking his wound, not allowing himself to feel the pain, and proceeding to finish fixing the car engine like nothing happened. Bay was quietly effective, strong, and stoic to the max. I was not. I tried to do what he did, but I have almost zero mechanical aptitude. I was destined to be a white glove guy."

When Mark was little, big brother Bay would sometimes allow little Mark to spend time with his buddies. "On a Friday night they'd all come over to our home to hang out. It raised my young self-esteem. Although of course, that was before I knew or understood what that even meant. Back then I could pretend I was a big, cool guy. I was basking in their respective togetherness and coolness."

At age nine something else happened with Mark, something that would foreshadow his approach to life from then on. By ten years old, he decided that he wanted nicer clothes. "I no longer wanted hand-me-downs from my older brothers," Mark remembers. "And most of all, I wanted a European racing bike."

20 Mitzi Perdue

1. Mark's Childhood

Mark with his brothers, Brian, Bailey, and Eric Hansen

He wanted a racing bike because he had seen racing bikes in Europe. In 1957 his parents had saved enough money from the bakery business to take the family on vacation to Denmark. What Mark remembers most from that vacation was being amazed and dazzled by the magnificent high-end bicycles he saw there.

Mark was only nine, but he set his heart on owning a luxury English racing bicycle. For a nine-year-old, that was a stunningly unrealistic thing to want. The price tag on the bike of his dreams was $175.

Think of any third-grade kid you know, and you'll probably agree that $175 is a pretty big ask for a kid that age. But it's actually much more difficult than what you might imagine at first glance.

Let's take inflation into account.

According to shadowstats.com, the dollar amount of $175 from 1957 would be equivalent in today's dollars to an almost unthinkable $12,547. Incidentally, today's top-of-the-line racing bike does cost about $12,500.

RELENTLESS | 21

1. Mark's Childhood

Something that expensive seemed out of the question. "My dad told me 'no' endlessly and repetitively," Mark remembers. "He couldn't afford something that seemed frivolous, enormously expensive, and an unnecessary luxury. He even asked me, gently and half-jokingly, 'Where is your capital? Where is your money-in-hand to purchase such a bicycle?'"

After hearing "no" enough times, it finally occurred to the young Mark to ask, "Can I have it if I earn it myself?"

"If you earn it, you can own it," his father answered.

This actually fit with what Paul Hansen taught his sons: "Pride of ownership follows pride of earnership." However, Mark's father probably never dreamed that his nine-year-old little boy could earn what would be in today's dollars, more than $12,000.

It seemed impossible.

How did Mark respond?

His response was an early clue into how he would spend the rest of his life. When faced with an impossible obstacle, he simply bent reality to accommodate his vision. He did it through force of will, coupled with obstinacy and an inability to think he couldn't do it.

By the way, this was something he'd do continually for the rest of his life. He made the impossible happen. It had its true beginnings, or at least it's clearly observable, obvious beginnings when he was nine-years-old, yearning for that expensive racing bike.

"The size of your question determines the size of your result."

Mark Victor Hansen

Mark knew he was going to earn that money, but where to start? Showing skills that would see him in good stead for the rest of his life, he did two important things:

1. **He figured out how to get from here to there.**
    - The "here" was, "I have no money."
    - The "there" was, "I need $175 to buy the bicycle of my dreams."

    The approach that worked for Mark involved sales. As a Cub Scout, Mark read in the scouting magazine *Scout Life* that he could sell greeting cards on consignment. He sat down with paper and pencil and created a plan to sell the Gibson greeting cards advertised in the magazine. He calculated how many he would have to sell to earn enough money to buy his longed-for English racing bike.

2. **He put his plan into action.**
    A plan is just a fantasy unless it's put into action. Even by this young age, the nine-year-old had mastered the second ingredient needed for success: He knew he needed not only to plan but also to execute.
    Here's what he did.
    His mother, who was a great saleswoman and storyteller, advised him to call on all the neighbors and share his story by saying, "I am earning my own bicycle selling Gibson greeting cards. Would you like one box or two?"
    She carefully instructed her pre-teen son to shut up and smile after asking his closing question.
    "I went door to-door selling greeting cards, expanding into neighborhoods I had never been in before," Mark remembers. "I sold 376 boxes in the two months before Christmas."

1. Mark's Childhood

The price was $2 per box of cards, and he got to keep $1 per box sold. "It was fun to sell," Mark recalls. "I discovered I loved doing it."

The $376 he earned was more than double what he needed to buy the racing bike. The additional money he earned led to another lesson, this time involving savings.

"Dad insisted that I take half the money earned, after buying my own racing bike and put it in the bank for my college fund. Dad couldn't clearly explain to me why he did what he did next, but over time I came to thank him for his action," Mark remembered.

"There was $201 left over from my greeting card sales. Dad took me to the Little Fort Bank in Waukegan, Illinois, and introduced me to the branch manager. He helped me open an account, and he made a big deal out of it that I was a nine-year-old signatory to an account with my name on it. He recognized that the money in the account was money that I had earned."

Mark finishes that story by mentioning, "Of course, I sold the manager a box of Christmas cards. The guy laughed, then thanked me."

Mark remembers the joy of walking out of the bank, clutching the red, wallet-size bank book, a grin on his face, and his father looking down at him with pride beaming across his face.

Seven years later, that bank account would help him start a project that enabled him to make more money in an evening than his father made in a year. But that's for the next chapter.

This kind of effort he put into selling the Gibson greeting cards resulted in his becoming the number one young salesman for Gibson Greeting Cards, and it gets better.

1. Mark's Childhood

Decades later and after Mark became famous for the *Chicken Soup for the Soul* books, he got an unexpected call from an official from the Gibson greeting card company (now American Greetings). Gibson greeting cards wanted him to negotiate a license with them to sell *Chicken Soup for the Soul* Christmas cards in grocery stores. "We sold 867,000 boxes of their Christmas cards," Mark remembers.

Mark's first experience with greeting card sales deeply influenced his way of thinking for the rest of his life. It foreshadowed the rest of his career—his willingness to go all in.

If you'd like to get a jump-start on success, learn from Mark's childhood experience and put his approach into action, take a look in the next chapter at how these attitudes helped Mark begin earning more in a day than his father earned in a year.

Learn from Mark:

- Self-reliance and self-determination in action equals self-empowerment. "When you set your mind on something and make a life-improving decision, you take control of your future and your life. You go from being a little cat to a big cat." He likes to say, "A big shot is a little shot who just keeps shooting!"
- Success equals both planning and execution. It wasn't enough for the boy to have a grandiose desire to earn the equivalent of $12,500 in today's dollars. He could never have done it if he hadn't had a good plan and the energy and dedication to execute.
- When you're earning, save. "Dad wisely took half my earnings and banked them. In later life, when I followed this

1. Mark's Childhood

advice, I did great. When I forgot it, which I did in my teens, I paid for it. Part of all you earn is yours to keep, save the first 10 percent of all earnings, gifts, windfalls, and bonuses."

- Use adversity as a bridge to your destiny. Mark's father couldn't afford to buy him the bike he craved. Still, this small event in the life of the young boy turned out to be a bridge to his growing, and expanding self-confidence and destiny. The same creativity and energy that enabled him to pay for the bike he wanted helped him become the "World's Best-Selling Nonfiction Author."

- Look for opportunities everywhere. Spiritually, ask the God-in-me, before falling asleep, "Where are my opportunities to positively earn money now in a way that is ethical, honest, and omni-beneficial?" There is always a way; it's each of our lifelong jobs to keep finding that way.

Mark with his Dad, Paul A. Hansen, ready to go for a bicycle ride

2 Teen Years and How Mark Became "The Beatles 2.0"

With his adventures in selling greeting cards under his belt, Mark had developed a skill for earning money and also a taste for it. In his teens, he continued this trajectory.

"Earning my own money gave me choice, freedom, and ever-expanding opportunities," he says. "I went to work big time. I shoveled mountains of snow from my neighbors' driveways, sidewalks, and storefronts. I washed windows in the spring and fall. I cut lawns, and of course, Dad insisted if I was to make all that money cutting lawns, I could pay for my own gas-powered lawn mower, and I did. I earned money doing all kinds of chores for the neighbors. I discovered that I loved to work."

Paul Hansen encouraged his sons in this attitude. As a hard-working entrepreneur himself, he wanted his children to value money, but he also wanted them to have a great work ethic. He wanted them to be able to make the best use of the opportunities that would come their way.

As he told Mark, "Free enterprise means the more enterprising you are, the freer you are."

He also taught, "Pride of ownership follows pride of earnership." And "You must be consistent, persistent, and

2. Teen Years & Beatles 2.0

insistent on your savings. If you will do this, you will be able to be, do, and have all that you can ever imagine."

"It made a big impression on me," Mark remembers. "I have likewise tried to share that wisdom with my children and my grandchildren."

Earning money for the English racing bike set Mark on his never-ending entrepreneurial journey that revealed to him what money could make it possible.

The bike itself created for him unending opportunities for adventure. A good many of these happened in the company of classmate and childhood friend Gary Youngberg. Gary already had a bike, and now that Mark had one, there was no stopping the two boys.

Thinking back on this time, Youngberg says, "After he got his bike, we used to go biking all the time. We'd just take off, and go for a ride in the country, and see places we hadn't seen before. I recall one day when we were out riding we came across a grass airstrip and saw a little house at the end."

How intriguing for a couple of junior explorers.

The airstrip was too small for a control tower, but instead there was a lady inside the little building, and according to Youngberg, she was sitting behind a desk, talking to a pilot who was up in the sky. She was using an old-fashioned microphone to direct the pilot to the landing strip.

They watched and listened as she guided the plane, which had been a speck in the sky. It became larger and larger, and noisier and noisier, until it finally touched the earth and bumped along the grass airstrip.

The pilot climbed out of his Piper Cub and, to the undying delight of the two boys, asked, "Do you boys want to go for a ride?"

What could be closer to heaven for a couple of eleven-year-olds? The pilot took them up in his plane, swooping around the countryside, letting them see familiar fields, roads, and buildings from dramatic angles they never imagined.

This exciting adventure eventually came to an end because the rule in both families was the boys had to be home before the streetlights came on. Youngberg continues the story. "I showed up home that night and my parents asked their usual question, "What did you do today?"

"I went flying in an airplane."

"You what?" his amazed father asked. Youngberg knew that being with Mark guaranteed that there was a continuous stream of fun things to do.

School, of course, played a major role in their lives. Gary remembers that neither of them were in any of the gifted classes. "We were both good students, but we had a lot of outside interests, and we weren't looking at our books all the time but we were 'A' students."

Mark may have been an 'A' student in most subjects, but he excelled at writing. He attributes his writing skills to having had "the greatest English teacher ever, Mr. John Reinhardt."

Mark remembers that the man who influenced him so much and gave him an undying appreciation of reading and writing. To Mark, he was a man who seemed bigger than life. "He was an elegant man, noticeably well-attired for a teacher. He was savvy, persuasive, informed, well-mannered, well-married, and a brilliant thespian. He took his act into the classroom where he inspired the students to find their genius and super-talents in thinking, writing, and answering questions. He got us to love reading, writing, and thinking our own thoughts. He encouraged us to debate him and defend our youthful positions, perceptions, and judgments."

Mark remembers how Reinhardt helped get his students through the trauma of the Kennedy assassination. "When President John F. Kennedy was shot November 22, 1963, at about 11:30 am Illinois time, I was sitting in Reinhardt's class. The high school principal announced what had happened and said that school was over for the day.

"Mr. Reinhardt asked each of us to call our moms and dads, but we didn't leave. We stayed to discuss what President Kennedy meant to us. Everyone stayed until 6:00 pm and even after that, some of the parents who were off work came to sit in the class and listen to this brilliant man direct us through the first major heartfelt tragedy and death that we'd experienced."

The students had all read, watched, and heard the music of *Camelot*, because Reinhardt told them it was JFK's favorite story. The part that resonated most was about King Arthur and the Round Table. Reinhardt told them that someday they'd be at the proverbial Round Table, and they needed to be able to think wisely and serve greatly.

"When it happens, not if," he thundered, then slapped his hand down hard on the desk. He was doing what Tony Robbins calls a 'pattern interrupt' for emphasis. He wanted his students to remember that each of them would have a 'Round Table Moment,' one when they would be called to think wisely and serve greatly.

Mark's attitude toward his beloved teacher was, "He deserved, and earned our respect, love, appreciation. He had our total enduring admiration."

Later in life Mark got to express that admiration. Fast forward to 1995. Mark and his co-author Jack Canfield won "The Book of the Year Award" at the American Booksellers Association in Chicago. Mark was allowed to bring only two people to the front of the audience of 60,000 book people at the McCormick Place Convention Center.

"My parents had passed," he said of the event, "so I brought Mr. and Mrs. Reinhardt." He acknowledged his teacher's profound and enduring influence on his life. "Mr. Reinhardt got the reflected glory and saw me at my first, and extraordinarily important, metaphorical 'Round Table.'"

Mr. Reinhardt instilled in his students a profound love of thinking for oneself and debating authority, in addition to learning to love words and writing. Leah Hall, writer for *Country Living* says, "It is the supreme art of the teacher to awaken joy in creative expression and knowledge." With Mark Victor Hansen, Mr. Reinhardt surely succeeded in that "supreme art."

Mark was doing well in his English class, but that didn't keep him from his out-of-school adventures. By age 16, both he and Youngberg had graduated from bicycles to motorcycles.

Youngberg remembers, "When we were on our way to high school one day, the roads were icy. We were going maybe thirty mph, and as Mark was going around a turn, he wiped out and hit his head on a tree. I rushed over to see if he was okay.

"I saw that his brand new, white helmet had a crack around three inches long. If he hadn't been wearing a helmet, that would have been it. Illinois had just passed a helmet law, and I credit that new law with saving him from serious injury." Or possibly death.

A happier event in their lives occurred when, at age sixteen, the two boys pooled their resources and bought a ten-year-old, baby-blue Oldsmobile. This made it possible for them to get a larger Sunday-only paper route in a more prosperous part of town.

The boys showed unusual conscientiousness. "We'd get up at 4:00 am," remembers Youngberg, "and we'd drive to the Porett Brothers Distribution Center. Our job was to assemble the different sections of the newspaper, and then we'd fill our car and drive around delivering them."

You might think that two sixteen-year-olds might quarrel over payments for their car or the work of delivering newspapers, but Youngberg states, "We never had any issues."

The next major event in the lives of Mark, Youngberg, and three of their other friends began a little after 8:00 pm eastern time on Sunday, February 9, 1964. It was an event that changed the music scene for most of the Western world. Along with seventy-three million other Americans, Mark witnessed the Beatles in their first American performance. It was on the *Ed Sullivan Show* and marked a new era in music. It changed the music world from Elvis Presley's rock and roll to the era of rock.

"The show was watched by basically every young American—seventy-eight millions of us, most of who are now Baby Boomers," says Mark. When the Beatles played "I Want To Hold Your Hand," Mark remembers being overwhelmed. "I was ecstatic. I was beside myself. My enthusiasm was beyond anything I had ever felt before!"

He heard the Beatles on the radio, and he was already a huge fan; one who bought their records as well as every magazine featuring stories about them. The performance on the *Ed Sullivan Show* was even more amazing.

Mark's response to all this? Mark did what Mark does. He wanted to do more than listen to the music. He wanted to be a part of it. He decided during that night watching the *Ed Sullivan Show* that he was going to create his own band and play this exciting, amazing, energizing, life-changing music. As soon as the show was over, he called Youngberg, and as Mark remembers it, "I screamed into the phone, 'Did you see that?'"

Gary had seen the performance and acknowledged to his friend that he too was beyond wowed.

"Great," said Mark, "we are starting our own rock group."

Gary asked the practical, nitty gritty question, "Do you play an instrument?"

"Uh, no. Do you?"

"No."

Mark wasn't about to let this little obstacle stop him. It didn't matter to him that he was forming a band without knowing how to play an instrument or, for that matter, owning one. He and Gary would buy the instruments and learn.

The next day Mark bought a bass guitar, since he identified with Paul McCartney, and that's what McCartney played. Gary got an electric Fender guitar and ordered the third electric portable organ ever to come to America. Mark then invited three other student musicians: the lead

2. Teen Years & Beatles 2.0

guitarist, Greg Simmons; a drummer, Eddie Gossar, and Skip Knutson, the lead singer.

Greg Simmons was known as "Killer" because he had a deep scar across his right cheek. Mark remembers that Killer had an unusual ability. "He could hear a song once and remember it, including every chord, note, or riff. He could then play it back flawlessly. He knew, and could discern what I should play on my electric Fender bass guitar, and he could teach me the chords. He was amazing and correct each time. Killer was a savant and a unique musical genius."

"We heard about, and went to meet, Eddie Gossar, who literally was alive to play the drums. When we went to Eddie's home, his room was decorated wall-to-wall with drummers' pictures."

Back row: Gary Youngberg, Eddie Gossar and Skip Knutson
Front row: Greg Simmons "Killer" and Mark

In a short period of time, the five band members acquired both a name, *"The Messengers"* and virtual manager Steve Cohen. If you were to talk with Cohen, he'd insist that Mark was the real manager, and he was more of a roadie; someone who went with them to the various gigs, as well as a friend and confidant. Still, his title was "manager," and Steve could get the band's groupie friends into gigs free.

Cohen's membership in the group was accidental. His good friend Greg Simmons invited him to hear a Saturday afternoon practice session of the Messengers, and somehow, Cohen hit it off with all the band members. He became an advisor, but his real job was that he was someone who made everything work. He was a year ahead of the other Messengers, but even after graduating and going on to Northern Illinois University in DeKalb, he'd come back on weekends to be with the group.

Cohen particularly liked talking with Mark. "Talking with Mark is following bouncing marbles falling down a staircase into rabbit holes. We would talk on fifty different subjects, and he was always just bursting with ideas, curiosity, and optimism. We'd talk about money and finance, or books, or writing, or movies, or anything. And something else important to me: we enjoyed the same sense of humor."

Cohen believes it really was Mark who deserved the title of manager. "He was the one with the ideas, who made all the phone calls, who did the advertising in the newspapers. He was the pusher and the one to say, 'Okay, guys, let's get back to work.'"

Something else that Cohen observed about Mark, "He was always the big person and the big thinker. He was never petty or small-minded."

2. Teen Years & Beatles 2.0

The Messengers assembled in a matter of days. Two weeks into the project the group had already learned fifty hit songs. Meanwhile, Youngberg and Mark each learned to play the guitar, starting from nothing. "We practiced like there was no tomorrow, and we did the impossible because we didn't know it was impossible and, might I add, we found it great fun!" says Mark.

One obstacle they faced early on was part of Mark's goal in forming a band to perform publicly and charge for it. To do this, they needed to join the musicians' union. Unfortunately, the musicians' union in Waukegan, Illinois, didn't want them.

"What kind of music do you guys play?" the head of the local union asked Mark.

"Rock!" Mark announced, beaming with pride and excited to be a part of Beatlemania.

The musicians' union guy was unimpressed. He and his cronies were Lawrence Welk musicians through-and-through, and didn't want the Messengers as competition. His gruff body language matched his words: "We don't want your music, and we certainly don't want rock!"

The musicians' union official came from the era that favored Lawrence Welk-type music. He was used to big band music. That style of music was pleasant enough but tended toward sedate.

The loud, enthusiastic, raucous, energetic Beatles music offended him. It grated on his ears. It was irritating. It was the proverbial fingernail scratching away at a blackboard.

At this point, Mark needed all the salesmanship skills he had been developing since age nine. Part of being a good salesperson is not being discouraged by a turndown, while staying diplomatic and being ready to persevere.

The sixteen-year-old cajoled the older man. "I told him we weren't competition or interested in the same market. We were here to entertain teenyboppers, probably like your daughter. We'll stay in our lane of music, I promise."

Mark reports that each of the band members pulled out the cash it would take for their dues, and when the union official saw that they had the cash, "He changed his tune and with a huge smile, he let us sign on."

After a chilly start, Mark and the union leader enjoyed a long and mutually enjoyable association. "Once we called on him to go to Kenosha, Wisconsin to help us with a venue manager who wouldn't pay us. The union muscle actually got us the money, but the venue manager asked us not to return for another engagement there—even though the attendees at our concert loved us and wanted us to return."

Within a couple of weeks, he and The Messengers were performing at local churches, clubs, and bars.

The next step was an agreement with the local YMCA to use their basketball court for weekend concerts. "I knew the court was empty during the weekends," Mark recalls, "and the YMCA is a great organization and could always use more funds to serve its constituents. I told them, 'Make it available to us for our performances, and we'll split the take fifty-fifty. We take all the risk. New people will come in droves to the Y, and it will be great for everyone involved.'"

Fortunately, the Messengers were able to draw sell-out crowds. They charged $5 per person and usually played to sold-out houses. Several times, for the YMCA, this meant a

2. Teen Years & Beatles 2.0

$2,500-a-night windfall and an equal amount for Mark and The Messengers.

Later, Mark learned this was called a "cause-related-charity" and made their performances a regular activity modified to suit every charity that he contributed to or raised money for. The result: everyone won and was delighted.

The band was now making serious money. Still, it took work to get good enough to earn this much. "We practiced every afternoon after school, and then started early on each Saturday. We made it a point to learn all the number one songs. We'd perform them every night and then get up at 5:00 am the next day to get our schoolwork done."

Often, the Messengers were getting as many as seven gigs a week. "We were smoking hot. Audiences loved us and would dance to our music until the halls, clubs, bars, or discos shut down."

Mark wasn't merely the guy who started the band; he was also its promoter. At one point the teenager risked doing something big-league, putting on an event at the local John F. Kennedy Convention Center.

The Center management doubted that kids this young could deliver. To reserve the space, they required the Messengers to make all the payments up front plus a security deposit. Mark was way out on a limb. It was a gutsy move because they could have lost thousands of dollars.

To help improve the odds of success, Mark invested in a full-page advertisement in the Waukegan Township High School paper. The ad cost fifty dollars, which seemed then to be outrageous. According to *ShadowStats*, that $50 would be around $3,000 in today's inflation-adjusted dollars.

Fortunately, more than 1,000 people showed up. The Messengers easily topped $5,000 in ticket sales, and in addition to that, they had the revenue from the concessions.

The money they were earning meant they were also spending. As Mark remembers, "We bought cars, motorcycles, and went to Broadway shows in Chicago and Milwaukee. We were the talk of our schools. Even Mayor Robert Sabonjian in Waukegan hired us in our senior year to rock the new beach front when it opened. Our lives were beyond thrilling."

Since all five Messengers were still high schoolers at this time, you might wonder what happened to their grades. Amazingly, their schoolwork improved. When studying in the few hours available, they focused as never before. In Mark's case, he went from being an average student to being an A student in almost all his subjects.

The Messengers lasted for the next two years until they all graduated from high school, and each band member went on to higher education. For Mark, higher education meant academic education but also, spiritual education, as we'll see in the next chapter.

Learn from Mark:

- If you can dream it, you can do it, too. . . if you put Mark's process into practice.
- It's okay to start with nothing, as long as you have a white-hot, burning desire. "When starting the Messengers, we didn't have instruments, we didn't know how to play, we didn't know the first thing about being musicians, and we had no idea how to market our product. But we learned."

2. Teen Years & Beatles 2.0

- When you really want to, you can learn things really fast. In my case, I needed to learn to play the bass guitar. The total time from when I heard the Beatles and wanted to form a band to the time I was performing in front of an audience, was roughly three weeks."
- Expect obstacles. "Initially, the musicians' union didn't take us seriously. They didn't like us or our music, and it looked like they wouldn't allow us to join. Still, they ended up being huge supporters."
- If you're young, you don't have to wait until you're an adult to start working on your dreams. "In fact," insists Mark, "when you're young, and you don't have a mortgage or a family—a wife or kids to support—it's a great time to explore all your challenges and opportunities to the fullest! When you're young, it may be your most cost-free time for taking big risks."
- Learn to live below your income. "Avoid the mistake I made, which is, with all that money coming in, I bought a great car, motorcycle, and scuba equipment. I went to concerts, traveled like crazy, and spent much of what I earned. If I had to do it over again, I would be much more careful. I would have learned to be a better money manager of all I earned: I would have saved 10 percent and invested 10 percent of everything I earned (or more). That way, the money I earned would make more money for me."
- Everyone has at least one superstar talent within them, but you won't discover it if you don't try. "I didn't know I could be a musician and a band promoter, but the act of trying made me discover talents I couldn't have imagined. You have genius within you—maybe in music, literature, invention, technology, or whatever—it's yours to discover and use. Dare to act and surprise yourself with the genius you have inside waiting to come out!"

3 Mark's College Experience:
Academics and a Summer in India

Take a moment to think about what your image of an academic is. In other words, think about a person who teaches or does research at a college or university.

Depending on your own experience, you may see in your mind a beloved professor you once knew, or perhaps an ivory tower kind of individual, or perhaps a sedate, contemplative person who's far removed from the rush and hurly-burly life in the fast lane of business.

I don't think you'd see the outgoing, exuberant, extroverted, charismatic Mark Victor Hansen in your image of a typical academic. And yet, except for an unlikely historical event in nearby Kent State University, Mark seemed destined for a career as an academic.

He loved academia, and he fit in surprisingly well. From the beginning of his university experience, his goal was to spend his life as an academic at the Southern Illinois University (SIU) at Carbondale. He was accepted at eight different universities, and chose Southern Illinois University because, as he puts it, "It had some of the world's most eminent professors, and the campus was so beautiful."

3. College and a Summer in India

The reason SIU had such eminent professors was because President Delyte W. Morris had a wonderfully practical idea for assembling the best possible faculty. During the 1960s, it was common practice for institutions of higher learning to have a mandatory retirement program. When a professor reached sixty-five, he or she was forced to retire.

That may sound shocking to modern ears. It was, after all, about as extreme an example of ageism as you can find. However, back then the attitude, at least in the United States, was that having people retire at sixty-five would make room for new leaders, and having younger leadership would create a more vibrant environment. This attitude was also prevalent in industry, and I remember my own father instituted this policy for the Sheraton Hotels.

Even though he was the founder and president of the Sheraton hotel chain, he didn't exempt himself from the policy. In 1963, he followed the rules he put in place and forced himself into retirement. To this day I still vividly remember how disconsolate and at loose ends he was when he retired at sixty-five. He died less than five years later. I think he might have lived longer if not forced to retire.

The retire-at-sixty-five policy was a hardship for those who didn't want to retire, but it proved to be an advantage for Mark's university. SIU *didn't* have this policy and President Morris, seizing this almost incredible opportunity, vacuumed up the academic stars from places like Harvard, Yale, Stanford, and MIT.

When Mark was a student at SIU, the campus boasted Nobel laureates, and an array of other academic luminaries. From Mark's point of view, the greatest of these was Dr. Buckminster Fuller, who in the end, was responsible for

3. College and a Summer in India

Mark's *not* following his initial dream of becoming an academic.

We'll get to Dr. Fuller in a moment, but first, let's follow Mark through his undergraduate years. His beginning was not promising. In fact, it was actually terrible. His parents must have been horrified. Freed from the constraints and discipline of living at home, Mark almost failed out his first quarter.

"I was drinking too much, and chasing women," remembers a chagrined Mark. "The Dean called me in to his mahogany-paneled office, and told me, 'Marky, I have your grades here. You got Ds. This may not be the right place for you.'"

The words hit home. By now Mark loved SIU so much that sometimes, he'd gaze at the handsome buildings, and the beautifully designed landscaping, and he'd think, "Holy cow, I've landed in heaven!" He wasn't about to lose all of that by flunking out.

He did something then that he's made a habit of doing ever since. When things were going wrong, he made a course correction.

"I was feeling like a dummkopf," he reflects. "I let myself and everyone else down."

He was tormented by what would happen if he were an academic failure. He'd have to face his family, and it would mean returning to his blue collar city to work for Johns Manville or another similar job. He knew this wasn't what he wanted out of life.

"Because I wanted to graduate college and become someone, I got serious about my studies. I stopped chasing women and made studying my highest priority. I decided I would develop in myself the discipline I needed to succeed, and I'd do it no matter what."

He was strategic about it. "I befriended almost all of my professors. I started hanging with the academically gifted. I went to all the extra sessions offered in the subjects I was desperate to do well in. I never once went to the Ratskeller, which was the name of the local bar. In fact, I can't even tell you where it is or was. I got so excited that instead of the normal fifteen units per quarter, I took eighteen so I could graduate in three years."

Mark started getting top grades. He majored in communications and did so well academically that even though the student body consisted of 64,000 individuals, Mark was known to all the top Southern Illinois University (SIU) student leaders, faculty, and leadership.

Mark even became close to Chancellor Morris and got to watch up close and personal how persuasive and innovative the man was. Chancellor Morris's foresight and leadership had catapulted SIU into the ranks of major American universities.

Mark felt that Morris's greatest gifts were persuasion and clear thinking. Mark absorbed many ideas and attitudes from Morris, but two that particularly influenced him were:
- Education is the surest way to secure a prosperous, meaningful future for our citizens
- Education should be available to all who seek it, regardless of race, nationality, gender, economic circumstance, or physical limitations.

As he puts it, "Education is the best way to advance in life." He appreciated that Chancellor Morris mandated weekly seminars for all freshmen to attend so they could be exposed to some of the greatest minds and thought-influencers of the time.

Mark attended three extra years without having to because he loved the idea of being widely and deeply educated. He enjoyed hearing the most challenging thinkers of that time. Great speakers and thinkers included the likes of Bill Sands, General Douglas McArthur, Dr. Benjamin Spock, Louis Armstrong, and over forty greats per year. "I even hosted many of them," Mark says, "picking them up, touring our great campus. We befriended one another."

Even today the educational values he received from his SIU experience shape Mark. For instance, the emphasis on the importance of education became the genesis of the Mark Victor Hansen Library that we'll be looking at towards the end of this book. To this day Mark has infinite respect for his alma mater and the influence it had on him.

During Mark's junior year, he was appointed a student ambassador for the Experiment in International Living. He chose India for what was supposed to be a three-week trip, and one of his motives for this choice was spiritual exploration.

At the beginning of the summer trip he met and became friends with fellow ambassador Byron Tucker. Tucker was representing Amherst College and the State of Massachusetts.

It was the beginning of a friendship that has lasted more than five decades. They both shared a sense of adventure and a passionate desire to learn everything they could about this mysterious, faraway country with amazing customs and a spiritual approach that was foreign to them.

3. College and a Summer in India

Touring India as a Student Ambassador with host M. K. Sreenevas Setty

The two young men spent almost three months in India, during which time they explored as much of the country as they could. They started out in Bombay (now Mumbai), and immediately decided to take instruction in yoga. Today most people know about yoga, but back then only a limited number of people in the US were aware of the ancient practice.

Yoga involves movement, poses, meditation, and breathing techniques, all designed to promote the union of our mental, physical, and spiritual well-being. The two friends were eager to explore this new approach to health and wisdom so they signed up for a class.

It didn't go well for Tucker.

As Mark remembers it, "The minute he assumed the yoga asana, or cross-legged pose, he popped his knee out of joint. The yoga instructor, not used to training inexperienced Yankee beginners, proceeded with the training. Byron assumed a more extreme Pranayama pose and collapsed in terrible pain."

Mark's best friend for fifty years, Byron Tucker and his wife, Liz

The bad news was Tucker had torn his meniscus. That's the rubbery knee cartilage that cushions the shinbone from the thighbone. In the cases where a torn meniscus doesn't require surgery, recovery typically takes six to eight weeks.

The good news? Well, there wasn't any.

The two young men were in a foreign country 8,000 miles from home, and one of them was unable to walk with an injury which at best takes many weeks to heal.

They visited a local medical doctor, but that didn't go well either. "The doctor's office seemed crude and frighteningly antiquated," remembers Mark. He can still see the one low-

3. College and a Summer in India

watt light bulb in the office. It had no shade, was hanging by a cord from the ceiling and barely illuminated the room.

For Tucker, it must have been horrific. A torn meniscus is painful, and the doctor hadn't given him any painkillers. But the pain wasn't even his biggest concern. How was he going to explore this wonderful, exciting country given the fact he was unable to walk?

Mark, with his twenty-one-year-old bravado assured Tucker, "Don't worry, I'll find a solution."

Mark's solution was to go to the local black-market and somehow find crutches. Since both the young men were about the same height, that is a little over six feet tall, Mark found crutches that would fit himself, tested them, bought them, and then triumphantly brought them back to Tucker. The crutches made it possible for Tucker to continue, and the two young men went on with their two-and-a-half-month adventure in India.

Tucker has a vivid memory from that time. "One day we were changing trains in Bangalore, wanting to go to Madras. I asked a guy who was standing on the train platform, 'Will the train that comes on this track take us to Madras?'" The bystander assured him that it would.

The two young men relaxed, now confident that they were in the right place. But moments later, they saw crowds of people dashing at breakneck speed to catch another train on a different track. From where they were, the track could only be reached by crossing an over-pass.

"To our surprise," remembers Tucker, "we discovered that the train on the other side of the crossing, the one that everyone was swarming toward, would be leaving for Madras in ten minutes. The track where we were waiting

48 Mitzi Perdue

did have a train that would be going to Madras, but not for two days!"

Tucker's knee was still injured, and reaching the other track would mean going up the stairs, crossing over the tracks, and then coming down the stairs on the other side to reach that track.

Tucker's knee injury was incapacitating. There was no way he could do this. Over the noise of the crowded platform, Mark yelled at him, "Get on my back!"

"I leapt on his back," remembers Tucker. "Keep in mind that I'm six foot one, and we needed to carry two bags plus my crutches. However, Mark was six foot three. He's amazingly strong and very determined. Carrying me on his back, the two suitcases, and my crutches, he sprinted up the stairs, dashed across the overpass, and then plunged down the stairs on the other side. We ended up throwing our bags on the moving train and climbing on just as the train for Madras was leaving the station."

Back then, men's and women's cars were segregated. The men were squished in like sardines, there was no air conditioning, and it was easy to recognize not everyone had taken a shower that morning. Thinking quickly, they jumped into the almost empty women's car. The women were screeching "Sab, Sab," and violently shaking their heads indicating that the two young men were committing a 'no no.'

"We acted like we only spoke German and humbly and respectfully asked: 'Sprechen Sie Deutsch?' Then we shut up for the rest of that train ride to Madras."

The reason the two young men wanted to go to India in the first place was they were attracted to India on a spiritual

3. College and a Summer in India

level. The purpose for their Madras trip was to visit The Theosophical Society Foundation, founded by Madame Blavatsky.

"When we got there, we purchased books, talked with the people, and tried to learn everything we could," says Mark. "We truly wanted to meet the purportedly five-hundred-year-old man who was living there, but they would not introduce us. We were considered naïve neophytes and not deserving of such a meeting."

* * *

After their India trip, Mark, and Tucker took different paths. "I went to business school at the University of Chicago," says Tucker, "and then on to Wall Street. Later, I got into private equity and then in the two thousands, got into the hedge fund world. Today, I do consulting with startups, helping them to avoid some of the mistakes I made."

Over the years, Tucker closely followed his friend's trajectory. "He was always motivated by wanting to help humanity. Initially, his goal was to provide affordable, easily constructed housing, carrying on what he had studied with Buckminster Fuller."

Tucker wasn't surprised that Mark became an author and speaker. "He was always a great storyteller, and he had a deep understanding of just how powerful storytelling can be. He knew that stories can focus your mind on the positive and in the process, enable you to create a better reality. His superpower is his ability to communicate a positive mental attitude."

> *"Positive thinking will get you positive results.*
> *You have probably tried negative thinking and*
> *what has that gotten you?"*
> Mark Victor Hansen

Tucker believes that Mark's understanding that we create our world by how we think about it had its roots in that trip to India. It influenced him for the rest of his life, and it added a dimension to his academic career.

Mark seemed destined for a satisfying career as an academic. He fit in, he loved it, and he did well at it. However, that was not to be his destiny, and as we'll see in the next chapter. Student unrest at nearby Kent State University meant that door slammed shut.

Learn from Mark:

- When you experience things going catastrophically wrong, see if you can change course. Mark was about to flunk out of college but changed his focus and ended up a 4.0 student.
- Explore the spiritual side of life. Mark's study of spiritual masters and yoga led him to a deeper understanding of life and how to live it.
- Pay attention to how much you create your world by how you think about it. It's an insight that can make you have a fuller, more satisfying, and more productive life. It did for Mark.

4 Graduate School and Buckminster Fuller

While an undergraduate, Mark became close to many of his professors. Dr. Alfred Richardson became his favorite.

Mark remembers Dr. Richardson telling his undergraduate physiology students, "Everyone here is going to get an 'A.'" That may seem like an odd approach for a professor to take, but it turned out to be highly motivating for the students. The students were inspired to study everything they could about physiology because it was so inherently fascinating, not because they were grubbing for a grade.

Mark would visit Professor Richardson in his office just to talk. Among the non-academic things Mark learned was his professor's philosophy: "Students first. Faculty next. Administration never."

"I adored this guy," remembers Mark.

Dr. Richardson turned out to be the man who deflected Mark from his proposed career as an academic. This was never Richardson's intention, but according to Mark, here's what happened: "I'm in graduate school," Mark begins his explanation, "and I'm hoping to be a professor like Dr. Richardson. I'm in his office one day, and he tells me, 'Cancel whatever you're doing the rest of your day. We've got a front row seat in the 5,000-seat auditorium, and we're going to hear the smartest person on the planet, Buckminster Fuller. He's a senior advisor to NASA.'"

Mark with Dr. R. (Bucky) Buckminster Fuller in 1979

At that point in Mark's young life, he was sure that Dr. Richardson was the smartest person on the planet, so of course he was going to do what his professor said, and accompany him to the lecture. Mark, however, was not expecting to learn much from this Buckminster Fuller guy. Mark's attitude back then could not exactly be described as "humble." Mark's own view of himself, "I was sophomoric to the max. I'm carrying a 4.0 average, I'm a personal friend of the Chancellor, and basically, I'm drinking my own bathwater."

Mark was a classic know-it-all. This was about to change.

Dr. R. Buckminster Fuller, was a comprehensivist, thinker, author of forty books, inventor, recipient of forty-

4. Buckminster Fuller

seven honorary doctorates in arts, architecture, humanities, and more. Bucky, as he was affectionately called, started addressing his audience of 5,000 with ten words; words Mark never even heard of before: "We're going to talk about cosmogony, cosmology, epistemology, sciences, systems theory, synergetic-energetic geometry, cartography, my Dymaxion Map, Dymaxion Car, geodesic domes, and how to make the world work for 100 percent of humanity."

Fuller's talk, and the ideals expressed in the talk were more exciting than anything Mark had ever heard. Among Fuller's ideas, one of the most exciting was that we can make the world work for 100 percent of humanity. "The technology exists to do it today," Fuller told his excited audience.

> *"All your desires and needs can be fulfilled, whereas your greed cannot."*
> Mark Victor Hansen

Mark's response? "My jaw drops, my brain is on red alert. I'm feeling all my life was in preparation for this moment."

After the lecture Mark went to Buckminster Fuller's office and begged for the privilege of being one of Fuller's graduate assistants. Mark got the job, at $200 a month. He could barely afford to live, but was living on the excitement generated by being with a true genius, Bucky Fuller. He was still continuing his graduate education, but then and there, he switched from physiology to design science.

It was a thrilling time. Fuller would give him oddball assignments such as telling him one day, "I want you to work out the superconductive cable to transmit energy cost-effectively around the planet." Mark is hearing this and thinking, "Oh my God, what the hell's a superconductor cable? And how's it going to fit around the planet?"

Mark and Fuller's seven other graduate research assistants began work on it. They were going through some of the calculations Nikola Tesla had already made.

Today Mark wonders if Elon Musk is also addressing the same issue with his Starlink technology of 40,000 satellites that can transmit information and potentially energy.

Mark's time with Fuller was so exciting that, looking back on this time Mark says, "When Bucky was in the office, I'd make sure I was there because I was addicted to being there when he was there."

One small fact about that time: Mark had so much respect for his boss that his instinct was to call him "Dr. Fuller" or maybe "Professor Fuller." Fuller insisted that Mark always call him "Bucky."

Mark's career working for Fuller as SIU came to an end under unfortunate circumstances. The immediate cause was an event that happened seventy-five miles away at Kent State University in Ohio.

On May 4, 1970, the student uprising at Kent State in nearby Ohio resulted in the National Guard killing four unarmed students. The nationwide revulsion over this event had repercussions that affected the Illinois university system.

Illinois governor Richard B. Ogilvie cut the budgets of the eight state universities, and Fuller's funding vanished. Fuller called Mark into his office and told him, "They fired me today, which means I have to fire you."

4. Buckminster Fuller

With Fuller, the most inspiring person in Mark's life ousted, Mark decided not to continue his academic career. Mark instead put into practice some of Fuller's ideas for using science to help all of humanity.

Mark's transition from academia to the business world was not without problems. One aspect of it became so dire that Mark wasn't sure he wanted to or deserved to live.

We'll explore these events in the next chapter.

Learn from Mark:

- If you're in college or graduate school, it's okay to change your major and your life goals. It worked for Mark to change from physiology to design science and eventually to professional speaking and writing.
- Outside events can have a catastrophic impact on your life plans. Roll with it! In Mark's case, the Kent State killings meant the professor who was his inspiration was fired from his job which resulted in Mark's being fired from his. These things happen in life. They're probably going to happen in your life. Being flexible is essential.

5 Bankruptcy and Finding His Purpose

Mark's dream after university was to make the world a better place by helping provide inexpensive housing. He wanted to build homes using Buckminster Fuller's design for geodesic domes.

Fuller's design involves hundreds of interlocking triangles arranged to create a half sphere. Homes that used Fuller's geodesic design were inexpensive to construct and could withstand environmental stressors such as high winds. In theory, geodesic homes could have created inexpensive housing for the world.

Mark threw himself into this with zeal. By early 1973, he had large orders and what promised to become a major business.

It all came crashing down in October of that year when the Organization of Petroleum Exporting Countries (OPEC) raised the price of crude oil by 70 percent. That move, together with an oil embargo on the US, came as a response from the Arab countries to the Yom Kippur War.

With the embargo in place, manufacturers making the PVC (Polyvinyl Chloride) pipes could no longer obtain the primary feedstock needed for making the pipes.

RELENTLESS | 57

5. Bankruptcy

Unfortunately for Mark, the large PVC pipes were an essential part of his geodesic dome business. It was these pipes that formed the interlocking triangles which were the basis for geodesic domes. What had once been a dirt-cheap commodity, plastic piping, became unavailable at almost any price.

The economic fallout from the 1973 Oil Crisis meant that Mark couldn't buy the materials to build his geodesic homes. Adding to that woe was the fact that people who wanted to buy Mark's geodesic homes were themselves feeling economic stress.

"I lost all of my contracts and two million dollars in the span of a few weeks," he remembers. "I filed for bankruptcy in 1973, and I was in absolute hell."

Bankruptcy was the most excruciating experience he ever endured. "I went bankrupt virtually overnight. In my twenty-six years of life, I never felt such mental and emotional turmoil. The bankruptcy was like a failing grade on my business skills and my future."

His self-esteem was in tatters. He was depressed and barely scraping by financially, living in a small house with three roommates. As he remembers the experience, "I was living in Hicksville on Long Island, sleeping in a sleeping bag in a friend's room at night, broke and penniless. To round out my dismal days, I would tune into the negative evening news on TV each night which only added to my depression."

As if going bankrupt wasn't enough, his personal negativity was causing him to lose his friends. "I was sharing and repeating what I heard each day on the news. People didn't want to be around a Danny-Downer. I was eating up all the negativity and believing that was the truth. I was at the lowest point in my young life and literally considered suicide."

> *"Problems are good, not bad—from a higher and longer point-of-view. Welcome them and become the solution. When you have solved enough problems, people will thank, revere, and ask only for you."*
> Mark Victor Hansen

But then something miraculous happened. It was proof of what Byron Tucker said that Mark absorbed back in India: "We create our world by how we think about it."

Mark's life was about to change forever. He would learn that attitude is indeed everything. "One night in stillness and desperation I begged God for an answer to the question, 'What is my destiny?'"

A still, small voice—Mark knew was God's voice—spoke to him, but not with an answer. Instead, it was another question; one that turned out to be life-changing.

"Mark, what do you want to do?" God asked him.

It was a moving and pivotal moment for Mark. Meditating on God's question, the answer came to him. "I want to talk to people who care about things that matter and make a life-transforming difference for them."

Mark understood that his destiny was to do this through public speaking. In Mark's mind, having a firm, clear understanding of his destiny was a miracle. But there were two more miracles in store for him that day.

"Miracle number two," he remembers, "was the next morning, I asked my roommates, 'Do any of you know

5. Bankruptcy

anyone who isn't a celebrity, or a white-haired senior, or a Broadway star, or a doctor or lawyer who's getting paid for their speeches?'"

To Mark's surprise his roommate John said, "Yes, there is a superstar motivator speaking this morning. He is probably a few years older than you but today he is cheering up all the downtrodden Realtors in Haiphong, here on Long Island. I can't go, so here's my ticket!"

Amazingly there was a third miracle in store for Mark that day. As Mark remembers, "I got the address from John, and I raced out to hear a guy who turned out to be a wonderful speaker and trainer—Chip Collins. As a speaker, this man was able to delight the standing-room only crowd of Realtors who came to see him. I watched Chip motivate and excite these people, enabling them to believe in themselves despite the horrific economy.

"He taught them how to raise themselves up to profitability and increase their individual performance immediately using his dynamic and easy to employ formulas. As I watched the session unfold, I understood how helping people improve themselves and their performance was my destiny."

Mark asked Collins if he would go to lunch with him. "During lunch I asked him to share some of his techniques and insights so that I could enter this speaking and motivational world." The response wasn't encouraging. "Collins told me the chance of my making it as a professional speaker was one in a thousand."

That didn't deter Mark. "I have a white-hot burning desire to make it," Mark told Collins, "Let me try!"

Chip was impressed with the young man's enthusiasm and was willing to share his techniques but only on the condition that Mark focus on the life insurance business which Chip told him, was a bottomless pit of people needing motivation. Meanwhile, Mark was to stay away from Chip's specialty, the real estate business in the five boroughs of New York.

Mark speaking at New York City event

Chip urged Mark to begin at once whether he thought he was ready or not, and that's just what Mark did. "Within two months, I was doing four talks a day. I did over a thousand talks a year for my first three years in the business," says Mark.

Early on, when Chip returned from a two-week vacation to Disney World with his wife and two children, he was astounded at the amount of bookings Mark had self-booked during his absence. They became Master Mind Alliance Partners and met every Friday afternoon from 4 to 6 pm to review what Mark had accomplished and what new problems and questions had come into view.

5. Bankruptcy

"We faithfully read one chapter each week from Napoleon Hill's *Think and Grow Rich*. We'd focus on how to digest and use the principles we were studying," Mark remembers.

Chip recommended that Mark sell his initial seminars for under their value, charging twenty-five dollars per one-hour seminar but also selling a higher-priced package of four topics that would benefit his audience: prospecting, presenting, good work habits, and closing the sale.

> *"Become number one in a small pond (a niche market) and develop and expand your number one status to even bigger ponds."*
> Mark Victor Hansen

Chip taught him a phenomenal closing line that worked to sell the hundred-dollar packages. Chip said, "Smile and ask, 'Do you want to cut the check or have your secretary cut the check?'" It worked like a charm. It worked so effectively that within a month, Mark was booked doing those four seminars per day. At one of their Friday meetings Chip said, "Raise your rate to fifty dollars an hour, and then in another month you need to make it a hundred dollars an hour."

What Mark quickly learned was he was able to bring immense value and excitement to the audience. With the help of his coach Chip, he learned that each of us can, with the help of self-help-action-audios, books, videos, raise our individual values and fees by ten times, a hundred times, and sometimes, a thousand times.

By now Mark had devotees who were getting results and giving eager testimonials. They were excited by Mark's thinking, his teaching, his words, and his stories. They were telling people that they were now selling million-dollar life insurance policies instead of hundred-thousand-dollar ones, and in the process, earning ten times as much money.

Chip told Mark, "It's time to consult on Saturdays, and charge a hundred dollars per hour, and have four agents come to you from 8am to noon at a restaurant with a private room." This new approach worked. Agents loved it and recommended other agents, and once again, Mark's fees rose and rose.

Audiences kept asking Mark, "Do you have that story in a book? I want to share it with my staff, spouse, church friends, or kids!" Mark did a multi-authored book titled *Stand-Up, Speak-Out, and Win!* It cost him a dollar for each book which he sold for ten dollars from the platform in front of small insurance audiences.

He sold 20,000 of these at ten dollars each, or a total of $200,000 in 1974. To him, it felt like $2,000,000, and his self-confidence, self-esteem, and self-image soared. The better he did, the better his listeners did. It was truly a win-win scenario. He went from little office talks to regional, national, and international life insurance talks.

> *"Each of us with high self-esteem, helps others create more self-esteem in themselves. Then, we all win bigger, better, and more meaningfully with impact. Ultimately, what you visualize, energize, actionize, you will realize."*
> Mark Victor Hansen

5. Bankruptcy

He then branched out to audiences specializing in real estate. Real estate franchises started with Century 21 in Mark's home city of Newport Beach, California. Suddenly, he was in front of audiences of hundreds and sometimes thousands. He was paid and could also sell every book or audiotape he produced and his earnings quintupled.

Something else revealing about Mark's career at this time: He became a founding member of the National Speakers Association. Just as he understood as a teenager the value of joining the musicians union, he realized that speakers joining together could inspire and support each other and help everyone be better off.

Mark in his office with books.
He has authored or co-authored more than 318 books so far

His friend Rita Davenport, a speaking legend and fellow member of the group that founded the National Speakers Association, understands Mark's thinking on this. "Mark likes to be around people who are up-to-date and who can throw around more good ideas in a day than you might otherwise find in a year." This was the beginning of a career that led Mark to world-renowned success with his book sales and speaking seminars.

Mark summarizes the lessons from both his worst year and his best year which both happened to take place in 1974. "I asked the question that would truly pivot my life in a better direction. I asked the right question, at the right time, to myself, to others, and to God." He now teaches this principle in the book he co-authored with his wife Crystal called *ASK! The Bridge from Your Dreams To Your Destiny*. "By doing this," he states, "you can pivot your life from distress and failures to abundance, prosperity, and your own inevitable destiny."

Mark transcended the setbacks that almost cost him his life, but he didn't do it alone. He had a mentor who inspired him to change his way of looking at the world.

Learn from Mark:

When you're feeling lost, confused, or like you've failed, here's what to do:

- Ask God to show you a bigger context for your life and for your destiny. Come to Him with humility, sincerity, reverence, and an open heart. It gets back to the Bible. "Seek, and ye shall find. Ask, and it shall be given."
- Ask yourself what you really want. The answer is deep within you. It takes quiet and it takes tapping into your deepest understanding of yourself. Fortunately, the act of asking has already put you most of the way to getting the answer you need.
- Ask others to help you. Somewhere, there's a key person who can help. In Mark Victor Hansen's case, the key person

5. Bankruptcy

was his roommate John who was available the very day Mark needed him. The Buddhists say, "When the student is ready, the teacher will appear," and you'll be surprised when you get to experience for yourself how true that is. Be open to it!

- The answer may be nearer than you think! Mark points out, "When we're devastated or stuck, we often think the answers are far away. But when you start asking, a radical new plan for you can immediately be delivered, and if you follow it like I did, it may lead you down a new path to the new career for which you are destined."
- Be the best you can be; don't try to be someone else! "When I was trying to be Buckminster Fuller, I failed. When I tried to be the best Mark Victor Hansen, I was on the road to my own success."
- Use your entrepreneurial excellence, planning, masterminding, and great thinking. This leads directly to bigger, better, and more profitable businesses.
- Work at your highest capacity. When you don't do all you are capable of—at 100 percent of your potential—you suffer, others suffer, and the world suffers.
- Make the most of your financial, spiritual, mental, social, and family potential. Mark's goal for himself and for others is that we all become fully functioning, self-actualizing, and self-realizing human beings who fulfill 100 percent of our individual potential.

6 The Ultimate Mentor, Rev. Ike

Mark's mentor Chip Collins, as mentioned in the previous chapter, helped set Mark on his path to speaking success. But Collins wasn't the only mentor or even the most influential. Parallel with Chip helping Mark was his relationship with the person who turned out to be his biggest inspiration, a man who helped not just Mark's career, but his soul.

If you were to ask Mark about people who've helped him grow, he'd rattle off a number of names: Dr. R. Buckminster Fuller, Bob Proctor, or Chip Collins. But if you were to take it a step further and ask, "Who was the greatest influence on you?" he would answer, "Rev. Ike."

Rev. Ike was an African-American inspirational preacher and evangelist who came into Mark's life at the right moment. In 1973, as mentioned in the previous chapter, Mark was not only up against bankruptcy, he was also dealing with the evening news and its steady diet of negative stories. The omnipresent negativity was bringing him down further and he was nearly suicidal.

It was at this low point in his life that Mark walked into Reverend Ike's United Palace Church in Washington

6. The Ultimate Mentor, Rev. Ike

Heights, New York, an area which most people think of as Harlem. "This dynamic young preacher's words burned through the dark clouds that had been hanging over my soul," Mark remembers, adding, "Something changed that day. A light penetrated my being."

Mark with Bob Allen and Rev. Ike before talking to 4,000 people at their Enlightened Millionaire Summit

Reverend Ike's words were a revelation to him: "God is infinite. God is rich. God created it all. You are made in the image and likeness of God, so you are heirs to the kingdom, and the Bible says, 'The Lord is my Shepherd, I SHALL NOT WANT!'"

"What powerful words!" Mark thought.

For Mark, those words changed everything. "The negativity, the struggle, the self-doubt I had felt in the past few months seemed to melt away. Instead, I was immersed in positivity and possibility. I even bought Rev. Ike's tapes with the little money I had left to my name. I felt deeply that I needed uplifting as much as I needed food and water."

68 Mitzi Perdue

6. The Ultimate Mentor, Rev. Ike

When Mark left the church that day, he took with him a beautiful realization—his life wasn't over; it was only just beginning. For the first time in months, Mark felt valuable, important, and able to create something wonderful with his life. He summarizes the experience by saying, "I had been baptized into a new awareness that would change me positively and profoundly—*forever.*"

Reverend Ike's sermons inspired Mark to sculpt his life through choosing the thoughts and visualizations that would manifest every single dream he had into existence. "I became a spiritual addict from that point forward and attended Rev. Ike's services every Sunday, often bringing friends, colleagues, and clients."

"I saw how Reverend Ike used his own mastery of the principles spoken by the Master Jesus, and the prophets of old. He extracted the amazing force within those messages, demonstrating true miracles for himself and others. He inspired his audience to awaken their individual talents, skills, and abilities.

"Reverend Ike believed that heaven starts now, and you could live each day in heaven or hell depending on what you chose to think," Mark remembers. "He taught all of us about the 'eternal now,' and that by changing our perceptions and vibrations, we could tune in to all the unlimited good that life here on Earth has to offer here. And do it now."

Mark realized that by changing our minds and hearts we can instantly pivot to doing what the Apostle Paul admonished: *"Be ye transformed by the renewing of your mind."* - Romans 12:2.

Rev. Ike also wanted people to truly understand the Bible as good news now and live a life of abundance as Christ

6. The Ultimate Mentor, Rev. Ike

taught: *"The thief comes only to steal and kill and destroy. I came that they may have life and have it abundantly."* - John 10:10

Mark's life proves Charlie 'Tremendous' Jones's saying that you'll be the same five years from now as you are today except for the books you read and the people you meet.

Rev. Ike changed Mark.

"Read books, listen to audios, attend seminars— they are decades of wisdom reduced to invaluable hours for you to instantly absorb, use, and effortlessly prosper from."
Mark Victor Hansen

As he states, "I can say without doubt, from the time I met Rev. Ike and absorbed the wisdom, philosophy, insights, and principles he taught, my life moved in a skyward-bound trajectory. I was a budding young professional speaker when I first came into the United Palace. I gained confidence, poise, and ultimately the stature and influence to attract ever bigger clients, and ever more lucrative contracts."

Rev. Ike and Mark became great friends and colleagues during the close to a decade that Mark lived and thrived in New York. When Rev. Ike died in 2009, Rev. Ike's wife, Mrs. Eikerenkoetter and their son Xavier asked him to co-write with Xavier, her husband's biography, creating and locking in his legacy. Rev. Ike has 28,000,000 active viewers on YouTube and had 20,000,000 followers around the world. The book is *Rev. Ike From Wishes To Riches: Exploring the Wealth of God-In-You.*

6. The Ultimate Mentor, Rev. Ike

> *"Ideas take nothing and turn them into something. Remember, thoughts become things."*
> Mark Victor Hansen

Mark was turning himself into a bigger, more influential person. In one brief encounter, he was even able to influence Mother Theresa and an uncountable numbers of individuals suffering from substance abuse. We'll see how this happened in the next chapter.

Learn from Mark:

- Don't wallow in negativity. "When I focused on failure and was saturated by the bad news that was inundating me from the mass media, I considered suicide. I know now never again to focus on the negative."
- Surround yourself with positivity. Mark recommends an inspirational seventeen-minute YouTube video with Mellen Thomas Benedicts. "The video describes Mellen's experience when he died for an hour and a half and then came back," explains Mark. "Mellen learned that here in the "university of life," we are to learn, contribute, and enjoy a rich and full experience only available to us when our spirits are in physical form.
- Your imagination creates your reality. "You have a choice about whether to think of scarcity or abundance, negativity or opportunity. Choose a reality that is upbeat and energizing and abundance-creating!"
- Pick the most inspirational mentor you can find. Mark feels that learning from Reverend Ike was a rocket ship that propelled him farther, faster, and sooner than would have happened without his mentorship.

RELENTLESS | 71

6. The Ultimate Mentor, Rev. Ike

- Your life is meant for abundance. "Your thoughts," says Mark, "are in control of whether your life on this Earth is turned-on and tuned-to the unlimited abundance that God means for you."

> *"God wants to talk with you. You need to start the conversation with a request—in the silence of prayerful meditation and then patiently listen... God answers in a still small voice that will inevitably become undeniable to you personally."*
> Mark Victor Hansen

7 Mark in His Thirties

When Mark was in his thirties he wasn't yet famous, but he was on his way. His friend Lou Tartaglia, M.D., has known him since 1984 and clearly remembers what Mark was like back then.

They met when Mark was a professional speaker and Tartaglia, a psychiatrist. A mutual friend, a minister, suggested that they get together. Tartaglia remembers that their 1984 meeting near Lincoln Center in New York, "We hit it off immediately. It felt like seeing a long-lost friend. We were talking and laughing as if we had already known each other for years."

Tartaglia says, "Mark had and has a gift for being as personable one-to-one as he is on stage." Like many of Mark's friendships, this one lasted across the years, and for many reasons. In Tartaglia's case, the bond was at least in part intellectual. "Mark's just the most versatile thinker you'll ever come across. Whatever subject you want to talk about, he understands it, relates to it, he'll give you feedback on it. Often, it will be something that he's already thought about and maybe even studied."

I asked Tartaglia if he thinks that Mark's being knowledgeable on so many subjects means he has a high IQ. Tartaglia's answer reveals his own deep Catholic faith.

7. Mark in His Thirties

Tartaglia attends Mass every morning and could imagine under different circumstances being a priest.

His view of Mark's intelligence is, "It's much more than having a high IQ or being brilliant. It's like the Holy Spirit puts ideas into his head. It's uncanny to watch. He'll meet somebody and he'll give them an idea that will enhance their life."

Tartaglia's impression doesn't end there. "Even more important, what Mark gets out of these interactions and what keeps him going is that he wants to help other people succeed. That's his motivation."

To Tartaglia, success is measured not by how much wealth you accumulate but how aligned you are with the purpose God created you for. By that standard, Tartaglia feels that Mark's life has been an unbounded success. "Mark deserves all the happiness he can get, and the reason is he contributes so much to other people."

Mark had an unexpected influence on Tartaglia's life. It began when Tartaglia wanted to meet Mother Teresa but didn't have the money for a flight to Calcutta. As a Director of Evergreen International Airlines, Mark was able to arrange for Tartaglia to fly at no cost on one of Evergreen's 747 cargo planes bound for Calcutta.

When Tartaglia met Mother Teresa, she asked him what he did professionally. "I'm a psychiatrist with a subspecialty in addiction," he answered.

Mother Teresa told him, "We have a town council meeting tomorrow about drug abuse, and we don't have any expertise in this."

She then looked directly at Tartaglia and said, "You are going to represent me at the Calcutta Town Council."

Fortunately, dealing with drug abuse was right in the center of Tartaglia's professional expertise. Within twenty-four hours of meeting Mother Teresa, this psychiatrist from New York was representing her at an important meeting in Calcutta.

There was a ripple effect from Tartaglia's meeting with the Calcutta Town Council. Mother Teresa was influenced by what Tartaglia reported and sent one of her priests to discuss rehab centers with the Vatican. This led to rehab centers in Italy and also in Mexico.

"Success is not measured by what you can get, but by what you can give." As Mark continued perfecting his speaking skills and aligning them with his spiritual values, he was in an ever-greater place to give even more. One of his employees takes up the story in the next chapter.

Learn from Mark:

- You can never fully know the ripple effect that can come from a generous act. Mark's helping his friend travel to Calcutta initiated a chain of events that have helped uncountable numbers of people in Italy and Mexico recover from drug addiction.
- "Being all you can be" means you can give to others on an ever greater scale.

8 Mark Changes a High School Graduate's Life

Lisa Williams is another friend from this period. Back then she was an employee of Mark's and today she is the VP of Marketing at the Jack Canfield Companies. She says her life could have taken a very different track if she hadn't had the good luck to start her career working for Mark.

It was back in 1985, and she had just graduated from high school. She knew she wasn't going to college and her father informed her, "You've got to get a job."

Seeing an ad in the paper for an office job with Mark Victor Hansen and Associates, she applied for an interview. Although there was plenty of competition for the job and although she had zero office experience, the interview went well and she was hired.

The job was to be a Girl Friday. However, at this point in her life Williams had no sense of vision and very little ambition. "I didn't come from a learned family," she says adding, "We didn't even have a library."

Associating with Mark changed her approach to life. He provided her a with transformative sense of vision and possibility.

He encouraged Williams to listen to inspirational tapes and even better, he invited her to attend the National Speakers Association where she'd get to hear giants in the personal development field such as Zig Ziglar, Og Mandino, Rita Davenport, and Cavett Robert.

Williams began raising her expectations for who she could be. "It shows the power of inspiration," she says. "I started taking on every challenge."

In short order, she graduated from being someone who got coffee for everyone to being the receptionist. Providentially for Williams, the desk in her new job meant she was sitting near Mary McKay, Mark's booking agent for speeches.

McKay's desk was close enough to William's desk that she regularly overheard McKay's phone conversations. McKay would be selling Mark's speeches all day long to the people who would potentially hire him. Williams got to learn from a virtuoso the art of prospecting, pitching, and then closing a sale.

In life, it often happens that when you learn a new skill, you find a use for it. McKay left her job with Mark to get married and, at just about this time, Mark and his then wife, Patty decided to take a vacation in Hawaii. Figuratively speaking, Williams was left holding the fort.

"I'm sitting at my receptionist desk, thinking about how Mark would be needing engagements when he got back," Williams remembers. With McKay gone Williams was still the receptionist but she thought to herself, "Why not use the skills I've been picking up by watching McKay?" Williams picked up her phone and began doing the equivalent of dialing for dollars, although in this case it was dialing for bookings.

> *"Make your now a WOW!*
> *Now is the only time there is."*
> Mark Victor Hansen

"I knew the drill. I knew what the meeting planners wanted. I started with offering free talks where he would make his money from selling books and inspirational materials at the back of the room."

The effort paid off and by the time Mark and Patty returned, Williams had developed a full schedule of talks for Mark. Of course, Mark was pleased on seeing this much initiative and promoted Williams from receptionist to a job she felt was much more consequential - booking agent.

In the years that followed, she not only got to watch Mark's business grow, she had the satisfaction of participating in that growth. Eventually, as Mark went from speaking to giving seminars, Williams adapted her skills to marketing in this new world. The seminars grew to mega events where there could be hundreds or even thousands of participants. Williams was in charge of it all.

"This period was a roller coaster," she remembers. "It could be frustrating and maddening, but his drive and belief made everything work. To this day, I don't understand where the energy comes from. I had never seen anything like this in my life. But I do know what drives him; it's a deep, innate desire to help people. His was a never-ending quest for growth and self-improvement, and when he learned something new, he always wanted to share it."

8. Changing Lives

Mark teaching at one of his Mega Book Marketing Seminars where more than a 1,000 attendees paid $1,000 to learn how to effectively sell, market, and promote their books

Although there was a thrill-ride aspect to working for Mark, Williams found it deeply fulfilling. "There was always fan mail coming, often ten letters a day. I needed to see this to validate what I was doing. These letters were proof that he was changing lives. We were helping people starting their speaking businesses, or writing their books, or growing their businesses, or becoming more professionally competent. Their letters enabled me to see the impact, to see the transformation, and I loved it when I read they were coming to the next seminar and bringing their friends. Or they would send copies of the books that Mark had encouraged them to write."

8. Changing Lives

The experience lasted twenty years but by the end of this time, Williams was beginning to experience burnout. Somehow things at the office weren't as exciting and sparkly as they had been earlier. She gave notice and only afterwards learned the likely reason for things at the office changing so much. It turns out that Mark and Patty were in mediation and heading for divorce.

"Mark and Patty went to great lengths to keep their personal turmoil private," Williams says. "When I learned they were in mediation, I thought, 'Oh, no wonder the energy was weird.' You could just tell that something was off."

As for the cause of the divorce? "I truly don't know since they were both so private about it. I do have the impression though that Patty wanted to slow down and maybe have a chance to enjoy gardening or traveling in Italy. Mark wasn't about to slow down even a little."

Williams knew that her resigning was painful for Mark. "It was partly a case of burnout, partly that the environment in the office had changed, and partly that I wanted to leave at the top of my game."

Mark himself wasn't quite yet at the top of his game. However, as we'll see in the next chapter, one of the ways he was getting there was a deep understanding of the following: *When you travel alone you may go faster, but if you travel together you can go further.*

Learn from Mark:

- Encourage your employees to be all they can be. Mark's encouraging Lisa Williams to be all she could be resulted in his having an extraordinarily committed and skilled employee.
- Draw energy from wanting to help people. Mark's energy comes in part from a deep desire to help people.
- Keep learning and then you'll have still more to share with others. Mark has always been eager to learn more so he can share his learnings with others.

9 Bob Proctor - Business Partner, Mastermind Partner, and Lifelong Friend

The late Bob Proctor was one of the greats in the speaking business. He died on February 3, 2022 at the age of 88. I interviewed him about Mark just six weeks before his passing, and we continued emailing each other until just three weeks before his end.

Mark and Proctor were close friends for almost four decades. Mark gave a video eulogy at Proctor's Zoom-held funeral. The funeral was a virtual one because it occurred at a time when Canada was still mostly shutdown due to the COVID pandemic.

The two men met because of an unusual reason. Mark's clients from several countries kept telling him, "You sound like Bob Proctor!" At the same time many people were telling Proctor, "You sound like Mark Victor Hansen!" They had a similar message: teaching people how to be more, do more, have more, and give more.

Since the two men kept hearing about each other, one day by mail, they agreed that obviously they should meet. In the late 1980s, they did.

9. Bob Proctor - Partner and Friend

Mark and Bob Proctor owned the Three Percent Club and The Million Dollar Forum creating predictability into becoming millionaires using our technology call "MSI" Multiple Sources of Income

It happened when Mark was booked to speak to 5,000 people at Jack Boland's Mega Church in Detroit. As Mark tells it, "It was a Wednesday night service. Bob knew I'd be there and called me ahead of time to say, 'I'll fly down from Toronto and we will meet.' When we met, we instantly recognized our like-mindedness and decided to work together."

The two speakers decided they could and should multiply each other's effectiveness by working together. They knew in this way they could do more to stimulate the spiritual and financial greatness in every individual they worked with.

This concept led to two successful companies: The Million Dollar Forum, and The Three Percent Club. In Mark's view, "Both were vastly successful, and our real triumph was the extraordinary successes of our attendees. We were creating millionaires because the attendees could change their personal mindset and, in the end, their future earning power."

> *"For the next thirty days, think, talk, act, walk, smell, and feel like business is booming and it will for you."*
> Mark Victor Hansen

At this point in the story, an interesting divergence creeps in. It's a divergence between Mark's view of how successful these programs were and Bob Proctor's view. The divergence reveals something important about how Mark's mind works, and how he processes the world he lives in.

His description of his ventures with Proctor is that they were a great financial success. As you know by now, Mark views the world through the lens of optimism.

As Proctor told me in a conversation just weeks before his passing, "Mark and I have been in business two or three times together. Here's one of our efforts where we lost money, although losing money was the least important part of it."

From Proctor's point of view, these are the facts. From his own experience and from watching other successful men and women, Proctor knew that to become wealthy, it helps to have multiple sources of income. Mark had come to the exact same conclusion, and the two men decided they'd teach people to earn a million dollars by developing several sources of income.

9. Bob Proctor - Partner and Friend

Mark, as a can-do kind of person, helped Proctor pull together a group of people with the goal of providing them with an over-the-top helpful, meaningful, and consequential seminar. It was *The Million Dollar Forum* at the Ritz Carlton Hotel in Laguna Niguel, California.

"We charged $5,000 per attendee," remembers Proctor. "Two hundred sixty people joined and it was life-changing for them. It put people on the road to achieving their dreams. Without the inspiration from the *Million Dollar Forum* most of the participants would not have half the achievements in life they have today."

The *Million Dollar Forum* was phenomenal in its reach and impact. So, what was the flaw? "It was a tremendous irony," admits Proctor. "We did nine of these, and we didn't make any money on any of them. We were charging $5,000, but it cost us $10,000 to put someone through it. We were losing our shirts. Here we were teaching people about earning money, and we were losing money."

In Proctor's world, "The real winners pick themselves back up and go on." In his view, that's what Mark does. Proctor knows that nobody bats a thousand percent and equally, no one is going to get it right every time. They lost money and yet it would be impossible to look at this event as a failure. That is, it could be counted as a failure if you only looked at the financial side of the *Million Dollar Forum*.

Judging the *Million Dollar Forum* is a question of perspective, and Mark as a congenital optimist, clearly takes the long-term view when measuring the success of this effort. Yes, it lost money. On the other hand, it created many dozens of millionaires, so it did achieve its purpose.

9. Bob Proctor - Partner and Friend

Looked at from a still broader and all-encompassing perspective, it created the world's most impressive publishing success. The stories Mark was collecting and the relationships he was developing were, according to Proctor, the genesis for the first *Chicken Soup* book.

Although it was Jack Canfield who had the idea for the book, the content that is the moving and redemptive stories in the book, were often based on stories that Mark was collecting.

While Canfield, and Mark were still planning the book, Mark and Proctor discussed the concept of putting together a book based on redemptive stories. Proctor admits, "At the time, I thought it was a dumb idea to put together a whole bunch of stories."

However, Proctor was wrong big-time, as he cheerfully admitted in one of the last interviews of his life. "*The Chicken Soup for the Soul* series led to the sale of half a billion books and a *Guinness Book of World's Records* entry for having seven books on *The New York Times* bestseller list at the same time. Mark and Jack Canfield inspired millions and millions of people to live more fulfilled lives."

Proctor has seen Mark experience both business and personal failures, but they always led to scaling still greater heights of success.

Speaking of personal failure and success, Proctor is well-aware that Mark's first marriage failed. However, Proctor sees this as yet another example of Mark's picking himself back up and going on. "The best thing that ever happened to Mark was when he married Crystal. She's a beautiful person. She's so good to him. She loves him and she is forever wanting to do things for him. He hadn't experienced

9. Bob Proctor - Partner and Friend

this before. She's endlessly kind and sensitive to him, simply because that's the way she is. You could write a book on how to treat people if you followed her. He is so happy today. He's really enjoying his life."

Jack Canfield and Patty Aubrey, President of the Canfield Companies and Trainings with Mark and Crystal

Proctor cherished his friendship with Mark. "He's one of the better friends I've ever had. He's generous and loyal, and if I were stuck and needed help, I know he'd help. He's frankly one of the best people I've ever known."

The love Proctor felt for Mark was reciprocated. As Mark said in his eulogy for Proctor, "I love, respect, admire him in all ways, and I am profoundly thankful to have shared a big part of my journey with my great lifelong friend, Bob Proctor. I have tears of sadness that he is gone and tears of gladness that he is out of pain and has, as he said in his final words, 'taken the Concord to Heaven.'"

In addition to the sheer joy of friendship, Mark's relationship with Bob Proctor was a force multiplier for him. The contacts Mark made and the skills he developed set

9. Bob Proctor - Partner and Friend

the stage for one of the publishing world's more impressive success stories.

Chicken Soup for the Soul may have ended up as one of the publishing world's greatest non-fiction success stories, but it didn't start out that way as we'll see in the coming chapter.

Learn from Mark:

- Work with people who can help you multiply your effectiveness. For Mark, working with Bob Proctor for four decades helped propel him to greater influence and success than he would have had without this "force multiplier."
- You can judge the success of a business effort by whether it makes money or whether it fulfills its purpose. The *Million Dollar Forum* was an enormous success for the people who participated, but for Mark and his business partner Bob Proctor, it lost money. Mark, as an optimist, focused on the people he helped.
- The real winners pick themselves up and go on. Mark and Proctor weren't deterred by the financial losses.
- Seeming failures can be the springboard for future success. For Mark, if judged by its financial performance, the *Million Dollar Forum* made money for the participants but resulted in losses for himself. However, the stories he heard and the contacts he made were the springboard for enormous future success.

10 How Soup Got Started

Mark Victor Hansen and Jack Canfield met at the Mandela Conference in San Diego in 1989. Both had given inspirational talks to the 6,000-plus attendees.

When they first shook hands, they immediately hit it off and with good reason. They were both not only established motivational speakers and successful authors, but what they also had in common was that they were both known as riveting storytellers.

In the human development space, they were in the top rung for inspirational speakers. They each had their own lane and didn't compete. Jack spoke primarily to educators while Mark specialized in business and religious groups.

Although they have a lot in common, Mark and Jack were also quite different. Mark was recognized as an outstanding platform salesman, while Canfield was famous for being more cerebral, a result of his academic background as a Harvard graduate.

However, the two men did have one more crucially important thing in common. For years people had been asking both men if the stories they were telling on the platform had ever been published.

10. How Soup Got Started

Everyone wanted to take their stories home in a book to their respective loved ones, clients, pastors, and friends. Parents wanted to share stories of hope and encouragement with their children. Managers wanted to share inspirational stories with their staff. Others in their audiences simply wanted to enjoy those moving stories one more time.

One morning when the two friends were meeting for breakfast in Los Angeles, Jack mentioned that he was compiling some of these stories into a book. When Mark suggested that they do this together since some of the stories were ones that he also used. Jack instantly saw the potential.

The goal was 101 stories that would enable people to benefit others by sharing stories about their lives. Remembering their motivation for writing the book, Mark says, "Jack, and I thought the soul of America was in pain and in trouble. What we discovered was that the soul of the world was also ailing and in profound pain."

Mark found working on the book with Jack, was in Mark's words, "A thrillingly enjoyable, and life absorbing experience." Initially, the two met in Mark's office but ultimately, Mark would meet Jack at his place an hour drive away. It was great because the night before Mark would read Dr. Jeffrey Lant's book, *How To Make A Whole Lot More Than $1,000,000: Writing, Commissioning, Publishing and Selling How to Information*, and then listen to Lant's audios en route to Jack's office.

Mark would be so turned-on with sales and marketing ideas that the first hour with Jack was usually invested in thinking about sales and marketing ideas. Right from the beginning Mark was aiming at having their work catapulted into the book sales stratosphere. "Mark brought to the table," says an admiring Canfield, "a never-ending vision that this would be a bestseller."

As the two collected more stories, they would edit and improve each other's thinking, perceptions, and idea flow. Mark valued Jack's editing. "Jack would find faults in my grammar or how things flowed and that was fine with me."

It worked both ways. At that point in their collaboration they affectionately called each other "Bubba." Canfield said, "Our personalities jelled!"

When working on the project, the two developed their criteria for what would be a perfect *Chicken Soup for the Soul* story:

- The story had to cause goosebumps, God-bumps, or chilly bumps—which we discerned as the visceral truth of the story
- Stories caused instantaneous behavioral change
- Stories were so compellingly memorable you could tell it almost perfectly after hearing or reading it
- Stories made us cry and moved us to happy tears
- Stories made us weak in the knees
- Stories changed our perception and paradigm
- Stories awakened our soul

They eventually collected 250 stories, and then they graded them on a scale of one to ten with ten being high. They also allowed for the possibility of a ten +++. Using the grading system, they narrowed the stories down to the 101 best.

To compile a successful book, they would need a great title. They agreed to meditate in their respective homes on

10. How Soup Got Started

the same night, asking for a mega-bestselling title before they drifted off to sleep.

What happened next is something very like what happened to one of the all-time gurus in the self-help field. Dr. Napoleon Hill's original title for his book was *How To Make A Boodle With Your Noodle.* His Philadelphia publisher positively hated that title and didn't hold back in telling him so.

Hill needed to go back to the drawing boards and find another title. Before falling asleep that night, Hill programmed his mind to help him find a bestselling title while he slept.

In the middle of the night, the title *Think and Grow Rich* jumped onto the screen of Hill's imagination. He called the publisher the next morning. The publisher loved it, and *Think and Grow Rich* has since sold millions of books worldwide.

The approach of calling on their subconscious minds to come up with a bestselling title worked for Mark and Jack. Jack called Mark at 2:58 a.m. and awakened everyone in Mark's home, plus eight sleeping animals who were there because one of his daughters was pursuing a career as a veterinarian.

Mark remembers what happened during the 2:58 am call. Jack said, *Chicken Soup,* and I said *for the Soul,* subtitled *Heart-Touching and Soul Penetrating Stories.*

Jack remembers that the idea for the name came to him because of an image of his grandmother's chicken soup. It was a powerful vision helping him remember his grandmother's loving words about how chicken soup would cure anything.

10. How Soup Got Started

With its elements of being a homey cure-all, the title captivated both men. As they discussed the chicken soup image further, the final version took shape. The book would have the same healing powers as chicken soup, but it wouldn't be for the body—it would be for the soul. Thus was born one of the most famous titles in all of publishing history.

However, in what became a recurring theme, not everyone liked the title. One of Jack's assistants quit because she thought writing such a silly book would hurt the company's image.

Further, potential publishers didn't like it. When Mark and Jack presented their idea to various publishers, there wasn't one who embraced the title.

Speaking of this discouraging time, Jack said, "Everyone was telling us, 'People don't buy collections of short stories.' And that was followed by 'The title *Chicken Soup for the Soul* is stupid.'"

Things were looking bleak for the two motivational speakers. As you'll see in the next chapter, things were about to get much bleaker.

Learn from Mark:

- Mastermind Partnerships can be amazingly productive. Mark and Jack energized each other. By thinking big, they were laying the foundation for a success that neither of them would have achieved on his own.
- Submerge your ego. The two men worked without ego in the sense that they would each edit and improve the other's work while welcoming the other's input. The result was a masterwork.

10. How Soup Got Started

- Meditation, or tapping into your unconscious mind, can be a formula for success. The title Chicken Soup for the Soul came after the two men agreed first to meditate on possible titles and then to sleep on it. The result was book sales in the hundreds of millions of copies.

11 Selling Soup:
A Case Study in Perseverance

Troubles with selling the proposed book, as well as troubles with its title, kept mounting. It looked as if things were on the right track when Mark and Jack were able to hire one of the country's top book agents to help them sell their book. Jeff Herman became their agent and Mark remembers personally liking him a lot.

Liking him wasn't enough. One day Herman told Mark and Jack, "I've taken you everywhere, and we can't keep working this hard for you because there's no traction. Nobody wants your book."

And then, to Mark's surprise, Herman announced, "I'm not wasting any more time with you."

"He fired us!" Mark says, disbelief in his voice. After all, how often does it happen that an author's agent fires his client?

Mark and Jack spent a total of fourteen months trying to find a publisher. By the end of those fruitless months, they had accumulated a close-to-incredible 144 rejections for their book.

11. Selling Soup: A Case Study in Perseverance

In Mark's sales training talks he taught there is always a buyer. He remembers, "We had one clean, four-letter word to handle each and every rejection: N-E-X-T!"

> *"Every time you get rejected, say N-E-X-T!!*
> *You will become rejection proof."*
> Mark Victor Hansen

During this time, Mark wasn't above calling on friends to get through this trying time. One was Jerry Silver. The two had met in the early 1980s. Silver was an entrepreneur, pioneering the development of cardiac rehabilitation centers. If you've ever been in a facility involving cardiac rehab, Silver has indirectly touched your life.

The men had a lot in common. "Mark was doing something very similar to what I was doing, in that we both worked with inventors. I helped inventors to commercialize their inventions, and Mark helped them by inspiring them to use their talents, and vision," says Jerry.

Mark and Jerry had, over the years, developed a close friendship. Although it was Mark who was the motivational speaker, he clearly drew energy from Silver. It's an interesting aspect of Mark Victor Hansen that even though, as an author, speaker, and mentor to millions, he has no problem drawing inspiration and encouragement from others.

During the fourteen months when Mark and Jack were struggling, Mark called Silver to ask, "What am I doing wrong? I met this guy Canfield, and we've got this great idea about growing through adversity. It could help people and I know it's important, but I've gone to dozens of publishers, and they all turned us down."

Silver answered his friend, "Come on, you're the motivational speaker, you can't give up!"

There's a lesson in that. As we all know, Mark stuck with it and in the end interviewed 144 publishers before he and Jack finally found a publisher willing to take a chance on them. The lesson is, even someone as energetic and persistent and positive as Mark knows the value of encouragement and looks for ways to replenish his reserves of courage and patience.

During this time Mark was doing everything he could to make this new kind of book attractive to publishers. He's known as a gifted platform salesman, but what he did next was audacious even for him.

When speaking before his audiences, he'd hold up a copy of the *Chicken Soup for the Soul* typed manuscript and say something along the lines of, "We have been turned down by twenty-eight publishers who told us this book wasn't good enough to make it in the market. However, Jack and I believe so deeply in this book and its message, we know the right and perfect publisher will show up. We need your help. I want all of you to hold in your hearts, in your minds, and in your prayers the idea that you'll see *Chicken Soup for the Soul* in every bookstore, airport, library, and school in our country."

Typically the audiences would stand and applaud, affirming his request and vision. Mark would then ask everyone to fill out an order form for the book, even though the book didn't yet have a publisher. He asked them to put their credit card number on the form and promised the book would be sent to them as soon as it was printed.

Talk about a bold and fearless ask!

11. Selling Soup: A Case Study in Perseverance

However, Mark's career was built with the help of this piece of wisdom: The answer is "No" if you don't ask. Mark asked and typically he'd walk away with hundreds of orders for the as-yet unpublished book. Peter Guber, Mark's friend who has more than fifty academy award nominations for his movies like *Batman, Rainman, The Color Purple,* and *Flashdance,* jokingly says that "Mark is so dyslexic that he thinks 'No' means 'On!'"

Jack was doing the same thing with the idea that they could tell publishers that they had already pre-sold thousands of books. "Before we had a publisher," says Mark, "we already had over 20,000 promises to buy with credit card numbers. Why? Because we kept asking and asking and asking."

Mark and Jack didn't give up. As we'll see in the next chapter, perseverance got them halfway to where they needed to be. It didn't get them the whole way.

Mark and Jack featured in People Magazine

Learn from Mark:

- If you want success, persevere. Mark and Jack demonstrated almost unbelievable perseverance. They
- When you get a turndown, the appropriate response is "N-E-X-T!"
- You don't have to do it alone. Call on your friends for help when you're discouraged. There's no shame in the vast number of turndowns they endured before they hit the jackpot.
- Ask for what you want! The answer is "No" if you don't ask! Mark got a head start in marketing Chicken Soup by asking his audiences to buy copies of his as-yet-to-be published book. Jack says part of their modus operandi was "asking and asking and asking."

12 Selling Chicken Soup:
The Ultimate "Don't Quit" Story

By 1989 Mark and Jack had logged in fourteen months of effort with nothing to show for it. No publisher had even a glimmer of interest in publishing a collection of very short stories by many unknown authors and with a title that was a turnoff.

Practicing the cheerful persistence they preached, Mark and Jack went to the April 1989 American Booksellers Association convention. They were still hoping to find a publisher and this seemed like Mecca. There were 15,000 attendees from around the world, including published authors, want-to-be-authors, agents, publicists, bookstore owners, and employees, and—this was the magic part—publishing.

The great and the famous of the publishing world were in attendance, and that year the VIPs included Stephen King, Dave Barry, and Amy Tan. Mark Victor Hansen and Jack Canfield didn't count as VIPs back then.

Since their agent had fired them they were now agent-free. The two men were on their own, going booth to booth trying to sell a book that nobody wanted and whose title was generally regarded as stupid.

12. The Ultimate "Don't Quit" Story

Jack remembers the time at the ABA convention well. "There were 16,000 publishers. Time after time we'd go to a booth, make a pitch, and ask, 'Would you publish our book?'" The only answer the two men were getting was "No!" "No!" "No!" "No!" "No!" "No!" . . . and then "No!" again.

The first two days were discouraging. The third and final day looked as if was going to be equally miserable. By the end of that day, the two authors had reached their whopping 144 rejections.

But then, cheerful persistence paid off. They came across a small publishing company, Health Communications, Inc. (HCI) headed by Peter Vegso and his partner Gary Seidler. Unlike any of the other publishers at the convention, Vegso and Seidler were at least willing to read the book.

Vegso had a background that made him more ready than most to read a book filled with feel-good redemptive stories. He's a pioneer in the field of self-help publishing and one of the things that sets Vegso apart from other publishers is that, years before he met Mark and Jack, he had made a commitment to be a conduit for good; to improving the lives of others. That commitment extended to every venture he would undertake. It made him open to taking an interest in a book that potentially could be a conduit for good.

Vegso's recollection of the timing of their meeting matches Mark's and Jack's. As he remembers it, "I was leaving for the airport and I hear some guy saying, 'I'd like you to read this book,' as he handed me a manuscript." Vegso took it and then maybe an hour later, while he was at the airport waiting for his flight, he started reading. "After the first few chapters, I was sitting there crying! It must have

RELENTLESS | 101

12. The Ultimate "Don't Quit" Story

looked strange to others, and I was worrying what people who saw me were thinking."

Vegso showed the book to Gary Seidler, his business partner at HCI. Seidler also thought the book showed promise. So, Vegso called Canfield, and said, "We can do it, but no advance."

An initial stumbling block for Vegso was the same that Canfield and Mark had been encountering all along. One of Vegso's editors looked at the initial manuscript insisted that Vegso change the title. The problem? It sounded dumb.

Vegso asked Canfield, "Where did you come up with this name?"

Vegso learned that Canfield and Mark chose the title because their vision for the book was that it would have the same healing powers as chicken soup, but in this case, it wouldn't be for the body—it would be for the soul. Now that Vegso knew the story behind the name, he decided to stick with it.

Vegso came back to Mark and Jack with the good news that HCI would publish the book.

"How many copies do you think you'll sell?" Mark wanted to know.

Vegso answered, "Maybe 20,000. If we're lucky."

Mark told him, "Our goal is to sell a million and a half copies in a year and a half." Canfield had the same estimate and remembers Vegso laughing in his face.

Vegso wasn't the only one who was skeptical. Mark's friend of forty years, the legendary speaker Brian Tracy, remembers Mark's telling him with his usual Markian enthusiasm, "I've got this great book idea! Jack Canfield and I are going to put together a bunch of stories. We're going to call it *Chicken Soup for the Soul*. It's going to sell a million copies!"

Tracy patted Mark on the shoulder and told him, skepticism ringing in his voice, "Sure, Mark, sure!"

Vegso told Mark and Jack that at best he could sell 20,000 copies of their book. If there were a Guinness Book of World Records entry for under-promising and over-delivering, what happened next would be a strong candidate. In the next eighteen months, Vegso published and sold 1,300,000 copies of *Chicken Soup for the Soul*. And that was just the beginning. Sales quickly jumped to five million, then 10 million, and then fifteen million per year.

Vegso and Seidler have earned a place in publishing history because of their relationship with *Chicken Soup for the Soul*.

Mark and Jack had different roles in the success that followed. "I was the business guy with a marketing plan," said Mark. "I interviewed the 101 bestselling fiction and nonfiction authors. These included Dr. Wayne Dyer, Dr. Barbara DeAngelis, James Michener, Clive Cussler, Art Linkletter, and Dr. Scott Peck, among others."

"I didn't ask them how they wrote their books. I asked them, "How did you market and sell so many books?'"

He repeatedly heard from them, "No one ever asked that," and then they cheerfully gave him advice.

Mark wrote down exactly what he was learning about how the very best went about becoming bestsellers. It became his business plan. Marks own view of it is, "It was audacious and outrageous."

12. The Ultimate "Don't Quit" Story

Mark was ready to use everything he had learned in order to promote the new book. He became the promoter nonpareil. He knew what he wanted and had a lot of good ideas for how to get there.

Mark has a lot of respect for Jack's work to promote the book. Plus he's a fan of Jack's writing ability. "Jack was a scholar at Harvard and it shows. He's a very good writer. When Jack finished the final edits, HCI never needed to hire a copy-editor for his work because what Jack produced was perfect each time."

Mark is not about to sell short his own writing skill. "I've been writing since I was sixteen. I'm a decent writer because I had the greatest English teacher ever, Mr. John Reinhardt. Reinhardt was bigger than life."

There's an interesting tidbit about Mark and Jack and their writing abilities. Later in life, when they were famous for shattering records for selling books, Harvard took an interest in how they did it. Both men were subjected to a vocabulary test to see how many words they had available in their repertoire. Both men clocked in at roughly 50,000 words. To put this number in context, readers of *The Economist*—well known for having brainy readers—typically have a vocabulary of between 20,000, and 35,000 words. If words are like paints, Mark and Jack have an extraordinarily large palette with which to understand the world and communicate about it.

They were peerless writers but that wasn't enough to sell books. They needed the right attitude. They became exemplars of Zig Ziglar's famous saying, "Your attitude determines your altitude."

12. The Ultimate "Don't Quit" Story

To get in the best success-oriented attitude, the two men took *The New York Times* Best Seller list and noticed that the top name on the list was Dr. Scott Peck. His book, *The Road Less Traveled* had been on the list for fifty-eight continuous weeks. Scott Peck would be their inspiration.

"We got a copy of *The New York Times* Best Seller list, whited out Scott Peck's name, and typed in our names over where Peck's name had been," says Mark. "Then we made dozens of copies and then posted them all over our homes and offices, especially on the bathroom mirrors where we would have to look at them.

Mark's Bestseller Book Wall of Fame

"Our theory was the best seller list we were looking at with our names on it would go through the portal of our eyes into the depths of our souls. When you do this, you take ownership of it, and it has to happen, because ultimately and inevitably, this is what your thinking leads to."

RELENTLESS | 105

12. The Ultimate "Don't Quit" Story

Continuing his explanation, Mark says, "When you focus on something sufficiently, it narrows your focus and you do the things necessary to get you there. You don't spend time on the things that aren't getting you there."

Jack had a similar mindset. He was and is clear that mental attitude, while essential, isn't enough by itself. He points out that part of the purpose of belief is to inspire action. "We did a survey of about 2,000 top entrepreneurs," Jack said, "and we noticed that one of the things people who win have in common is a bias for action. Taking action is part of the law of attraction."

In Jack's view, there's a danger that people may think it's enough if you just sit in their rooms, meditating and visualizing. "I always point out that unless you live at the bottom of a hill where there's a road, you're probably not going to have the Cadillac of your dreams come to a stop outside your door."

Both men agree that the writing is only ten percent of the job. Mark in particular focused on the fact that if the goal was creating a best seller, he had to hustle to sell books. He also knew that he needed to ask the Divine Mind for answers on how to do this.

Mark's attitude is, "You don't get what you deserve. You get what you ask for."

In the next chapter, we'll see how this played out. When the book first came out, it bombed. Find out what Mark and Jack did to change this and in the process, make themselves multi-multi-millionaires while making publishing history.

Learn from Mark:

- The successful person translates his or her goals into doable daily projects with deadlines, benchmarks, resources, and accountabilities, and then applies single-minded, wholehearted thinking to drive those projects to completion.
- If you're willing to decide what you want, believe it's possible, consciously envision the future, feel the feelings of what it would feel like if you'd achieved this goal, you can have anything.
- Being willing to persevere pays off. In Mark's and Jack's case, not giving up meant that today, books in the Chicken Soup series have sold more than 500,000,000 copies in forty-seven languages, and, together with spin-offs, have resulted in a billion dollars in sales.

> *"What's possible, exceeds what's impossible. Think about it. Do all you can do that is possible today, and in your tomorrows, what is impossible will be possible."*
> Mark Victor Hansen

13 Selling Chicken Soup to the Public

By June 28, 1993, and after getting 144 rejections from publishers, *Chicken Soup for the Soul* finally had a publisher. *Chicken Soup for the Soul* books were rolling off the printing presses and heading toward publishing history. It should have been a time of maximum satisfaction and fulfillment for Mark Victor Hansen and Jack Canfield. It wasn't.

The skeptics who had predicted that a collection of stories in a book with a stupid title wouldn't sell were initially right. The book was bombing. It got no more traction with the public than it had with the 144 publishers who had already turned it down. Further, they weren't getting media attention or celebrity endorsements. It was looking as if Mark and Jack couldn't even give it away.

Barnes and Noble sold eighty copies the first week, which is not a large number. Vegso remembers talking with Barnes and Noble, asking them to load up for Christmas. They turned him down.

It seemed as if the skeptics were indeed right. During this time, sophisticated and knowledgeable people were almost universal in slamming the book. They said it was too sentimental, too syrupy, and too "nicey-nicey."

How did Mark and Jack cope with what could have looked like certain failure?

Some critics say the two men didn't deserve the staggering success that later came their way. Their critics are probably unaware of how dismal the initials prospects seemed and how hard the two men worked to create their eventual success. As Jack Canfield often says in his talks, the two men were living examples of how cheerful persistence can lead to success. It's a case study on why the winners in life are those who don't give up.

> *"Great people are great because they solve countless, seemingly unsolvable problems—change your mind, think like a solution finder—like Elon Musk—and manifest your enormous, untapped potentials."*
> Mark Victor Hansen

Mark's good friend Brian Tracy, the one who was certain that Mark was exaggerating when Mark told him he expected to sell a million copies, takes up the story. As a fellow speaker Tracy got to watch as Mark and Jack gave away the books at conferences where they were speaking. He also witnessed something totally unexpected. People who received free copies began to buy copies for their friends.

"It started to take off," marvels Tracy. "It was 'getting legs,' and booksellers were starting to reorder." The reorders are all-important because it meant that the bookstores weren't stuck with unsold copies. "In the world of book selling," Tracy explains, "everything is done on consignment.

13. Selling Chicken Soup to the Public

If the retail customer doesn't buy, nobody gets paid."

Tracy goes on to share an insider fact about bookselling. "For booksellers, the most terrifying word in the English language is 'remainders.' These are the books that didn't sell and end up going back to the publisher's warehouse. From there they usually go the landfill. This happens to eighty percent of published books."

The average new book sells 1,200 copies. It's a fact of life that the top selling ten percent of books pay for all the books that lost money. That means that the majority of books lose money.

Initially every sign indicated that *Chicken Soup for the Soul* was going to be in the eighty percent of books that just don't make it category. Its destiny seemed to be, "We're heading for the landfill."

Jack and Mark devoted pretty much everything that was in them to surmounting those odds. In addition to giving away books, they had a staggering interview schedule. Typically, when they'd get together each day, they'd spend an hour or more pitching radio stations all over the country asking to be on their shows. Back in the 1990s, radio was the most effective tool for selling books. Usually, they each booked at least two radio interviews a day, and often five. "It was an incredible uphill slog," as Tracy describes it.

Something that kept the two going was, as Mark confided to Tracy, the mindset that they both had given during seminars on how important it is to sell aggressively and be persistent. The two partners knew that they didn't have a choice. They had to practice what they were preaching.

Slowly, the book was getting word-of-mouth promotion

13. Selling Chicken Soup to the Public

from ordinary people. Someone might hear Mark or Canfield on the radio. They'd buy the book, love it, and soon enough, they'd be returning to buy five or ten additional copies for friends and family.

Something surprising was happening. To use another publishing term, the "pass-alongs," were unprecedented. Repeatedly, a person bought the book after hearing Jack or Mark on the radio and then they'd buy several to pass along to their friends. The people receiving the books would buy additional ones for still more pass-alongs. Word-of-mouth from ordinary people meant ever-increasing sales.

Jack, not being a hyper-extroverted promoter himself, marveled at Mark's tenacity in sales situations. "One day we were at a mall for a book signing, but a few minutes before it was to begin there wasn't a single person there for the signing. Mark walked around the mall telling strangers, "Jack Canfield and Mark Victor Hansen are going to be signing books over there in just a couple of minutes. You don't want to miss it!"

Pretty soon a crowd gathered and the co-authors started signing books. Jack laughingly remembers one of the people in the audience looking at Mark and commenting, "Say, aren't you the same guy we saw in the mall?" Mark wasn't phased.

With efforts like this, the sales continued to mount.

Another factor appeared that nobody could have predicted. It came in the form of a member of one of Mark's audiences when he was doing his usual Sunday thing as guest speaker at a church. The consequences were enormous.

It was late 1993, and congregation-member Cathy Bliss

13. Selling Chicken Soup to the Public

turned out to be the right person in the right place, both for herself and for the two Chicken Soup authors. She played a providential role in the sales of *Chicken Soup for the Soul*.

For something providential, it's appropriate that this event began in a church, the Unity Church in San Diego. Back then Cathy herself wasn't particularly religious.

She was brought up in the Jewish faith but decided that attending a church with great youth group services would be a good way for her home-schooled kids to have a social life.

That's why she had started attending Unity. She soon found that she really resonated with Reverend Wendy Craig-Purcell. From then on Bliss almost never missed a service.

One day in late 1993, Mark Victor Hansen was a guest speaker at her church. Listening to Mark, Bliss was so excited about the stories of hope that Mark was sharing from his new book that, as she puts it, "I was ready to jump out of my chair."

At the end of the talk people were lining up to speak with Mark, telling him about how much they loved what he had to say and asking him, "Please sign my book." When it came to Bliss's turn in line she didn't talk about how much she liked the sermon. No, it was, "I think I can find ways to promote your book in my market."

Her market was selling books in schools. Mark's focus became riveted on her with what she remembers felt like electrifying force. "I could feel his entire energy radiating toward me."

"If you can sell 100,000 books," Mark told her, "I'm

taking you with me to Hawaii. If it's 200,000, I'm taking your whole family!"

For Bliss selling that many books seemed about as likely as winning the lottery—without having bought a ticket. Still, she decided to try for it.

The next day she called her employer Earl Kaplan, owner of Books Are Fun, and got permission to test the Chicken Soup book in local schools. Her approach to testing whether a book would sell was that she'd leave a copy in the teachers' lounge, along with the ten other titles in that month's offering. She did this in several schools, along with order forms.

An immediate obstacle involved timing. When she got her boss on the phone he was in the process of boarding a plane for Germany and couldn't talk. He said to do it, but as for how to do it, Bliss was on her own.

She phoned Mark but learned that testing would be a problem because the $7 price at which the publisher would make copies available to the author was way too high. Financially, it just couldn't work. Her boss was going to be away for weeks so she couldn't check with him.

Mark frequently says, "Someone on fire is better than someone with a plan," and Bliss proved it. On her own initiative, she called publisher Vegso and told him, "I can't afford the $7 price for the test in schools. I need to get them for two cents on the dollar, and I need two hundred. And I need to pay for them with a thirty-day note." This was an unprecedented approach, but to her delight, Vegso went along with it.

A problem that Bliss had to deal with was the original

13. Selling Chicken Soup to the Public

Chicken Soup had a black-and-white cover. How to get anyone's attention? For all two hundred books, Bliss hand wrote yellow Post-It notes with the message, "Love this book, please read it!" And then signed it, "Your Book Lady, Cathy." Then, on the top of each book, she also included a Post-It directing people to a chapter that would be important to them, "Why I Am a Teacher."

The economics of selling books to schoolteachers is, if you sell one book for each book you leave at the school, it's worth it. Selling two books for each one is a home run. To Bliss's unending delight, she was getting orders for five books for each book she left at the different schools. The test was officially a success. Kaplan arranged to have the Books Are Fun one hundred or so representatives throughout the company begin selling *Chicken Soup*.

It got better. Many of the schools started asking, "Can we get it in Spanish?" Bliss called Vegso, armed with information on the Spanish-speaking demographics for California, Texas, and Florida. Vegso felt it was a go but his next phone call to her opened with, "Uh oh!"

"I was hearing that 'Uh oh,'" remembers Bliss. "It's something you don't want to hear from your hairdresser, and it's something you definitely don't want to hear from someone you're doing business with."

The "Uh oh" worrying Vegso was that there are three versions of Spanish they would have to deal with: Castilian, Cuban, and Mexican. They couldn't afford to print three versions. Bliss did some research and found that there is a universally accepted version of Spanish. With that problem solved, Vegso quickly published the first Spanish version.

The next obstacle Bliss needed to address was that the

schools would be closing for the summer. "I didn't want to take two whole months off," she says, "so I asked myself, 'What if we create a book fair for a big company? They could use it to raise money for their favorite charity, and we'd continue to sell books during what would normally be a down time.'"

The book fair idea worked so well that Books Are Fun created a new division to handle book fairs. She eventually sold 400,000 copies of *Chicken Soup*.

Cathy and her family did get their trip to Hawaii, and for Mark, the chance—or was it providence—meeting with Cathy Bliss played a major role in turning the sales of *Chicken Soup* from a looming disaster into a major success.

Mark's longtime friend Somers White has an evaluation of what it is about Mark that enabled him to persevere and finally achieve success. White is one of the legends in the speaking business, and he was a founding member of the National Speaker's Association back in 1973. His friendship with Mark dates to this time.

One of the things that White observes about Mark is, "Successful people do the things that unsuccessful people are not willing to do. In the case of Mark and his co-author Jack Canfield, if they could get a radio interview for 6:30 am New York time that meant being ready at 3:30 am California time. They'd eagerly get up at 3 am to do it."

In White's opinion, "They almost killed themselves with how hard they worked to sell *Chicken Soup*." White feels that people who are jealous that Mark and Canfield have sold more than half a billion books wouldn't be if they knew the price in hard work and personal sacrifice it took

13. Selling Chicken Soup to the Public

to get there.

I asked for a summary of what characteristics led to Mark's successes in life. White didn't answer directly, but he did say, "We are all a combination of our strengths and weaknesses, and sometimes a bad quality is a good quality carried to excess." The comments below don't apply just to selling *Chicken Soup* but to Mark's entire life so far.

White puts the following in Mark's strength column:
- Limitless energy
- Willingness to work hard
- Resiliency
- Ability to deliver hope
- Marriage to Crystal

On this last bullet point, White states, "I've never seen a guy who makes his wife a partner as much as Mark does with Crystal."

In Mark's weakness column White puts:
- A tendency to over-exuberance
- A tendency to run after the new, shiny thing
- Not making his first wife as much a partner as he did Crystal

Thanks to the book's pass-along prowess, by September of 1994, *Chicken Soup for the Soul* was on every major bestseller list in the US and Canada. What was it about Mark that made him able to do this? The answer has to do with hustling. Mark is a hustler, in the sense that he works rapidly and tirelessly.

13. Selling Chicken Soup to the Public

Mark and Jack were on their way to success, but it wasn't a straight line. In the next chapter, we'll learn some zigs and zags along the way.

Learn from Mark:

- Develop, and nurture your enthusiasm! Mark is a 29,466 on the enthusiasm scale that goes from 1 to 10. As the New Zealand philosopher Henry Chester said 100 years ago, "Enthusiasm is the greatest asset in the world. It beats money and power and influence. It's no more or less than faith in action."
- Don't quit. If Mark had quit when things looked discouraging, he wouldn't have had the most successful nonfiction books in history.

14 Chicken Soup Sales Make History

By September of 1994, *Chicken Soup for the Soul* was on almost every major bestseller list in the US and Canada. Looking back on this period, Brian Tracy feels that the initial stages of watching Mark and Jack try to sell the book was like watching someone try to start an old-fashioned outboard motor.

"You yank as hard as you can on the pull cord, pulling it all the way out, and then . . . nothing. You try again and again and again and then suddenly, if you're lucky, you hear the engine chugging to life." Once the little engine that was *Chicken Soup* chugged to life, the book started to sell at a volume never seen in the history of publishing.

Tracy sees this success stemming partly from the fact that the book is good and partly because Mark is a genius at promotion. "Mark is a hustler, in the sense that he hustles. He works and sells and promotes and never gives up. The man is always positive and optimistic no matter what."

Tracy sums up his friend's success by saying, "You could look at what happened from the outside and say, 'Geez, he sure was lucky!' But to get to this success, Mark poured his heart and his finances into it and he never quit."

14. Chicken Soup Sales Make History

Chicken Soup for the Soul was doing brilliantly, but to Mark's intense consternation, *The New York Times* didn't include the book on its best seller list. To Mark this didn't make sense. After all, they were selling tens of thousands of books a week and yet *The New York Times* didn't consider them a bestseller? Mark researched who oversaw this decision and he immediately called her to ask about this anomaly.

"We don't list books that are compilations," she informed him. "They're not literary enough."

"What about the Bible?" he challenged her.

The analogy made sense to her, and soon Soup was on its way to the top of *The New York Times* Best Seller list.

Kyle Wilson is another man who got to witness some of what it took to make *Chicken Soup for the Soul* an historic success. Mark's friendship with Wilson dates back to this period, 1994 to be exact. Wilson still remembers when he first met Mark. It was instantly clear to Wilson that Mark wasn't a melt-in-the-crowd kind of guy. "There he was, wearing a purple jacket, bright tie, and telling the receptionist that she belongs on TV! Mark had a big, bold, stand-out personality, and we hit it off immediately."

By the way, Mark refers to Kyle Wilson as one of the wisest and most brilliant marketing consultants in the world. Wilson, before selling his companies in 2007, had more than a million subscribers and produced and/or published over a hundred hours of DVD and CD programs. In the personal development field, Wilson was a force to be reckoned with.

He began booking Mark for the mega events Wilson was famous for. He would often pair Mark at events with personal development legend Jim Rohn. As Rohn said of

14. Chicken Soup Sales Make History

Mark, "He was a category five hurricane that would blow things up . . . in a good way!'"

Mark loves answering questions from his audiences

The pairing was great because Rohn was brilliant as a speaker but his approach was a bit more thoughtful, a bit more cerebral. Mark provided a great balance with humor and joy. The audience got to learn while at the same time Mark, with his larger-than-life personality, delighted and entertained them. Audiences enjoyed the contrast and the different energy levels. It's a principle of speaking that you can't have a conference that's all whispering or one that's all shouting. Audiences enjoyed the change of pace.

The speaking engagements helped enormously with sales. As Mark remembers it, "Every time Jack and I appeared on stage talking and sharing our stories, we enjoyed a table-rush of sales that was beyond compare. Our book became the gift book phenomenon of all time."

14. Chicken Soup Sales Make History

By the anniversary of their first American Booksellers Association meeting, book sales were beginning to take off. Mark realized that a missing piece in their efforts to sell millions of books was they needed to get a great publicist.

"How to get the best publicist?" Mark wondered.

His answer was, "I asked everyone who had a bestseller. 'Who is the top publicist in the world?' The name that kept coming up was Rick Frishman."

Mark tried to phone Frishman. However, Frishman wouldn't take his call. Mark tried again and again, always with the same result.

Mark has a deep intuitive understanding of the importance of promotion. He knows that successful sales depend on people knowing that you're there. People don't buy what they don't know exists. Ideally, if your goal is selling something, you would like to be top-of-mind for anyone who is making purchasing decisions. Mark therefore wasn't about to let unanswered phone calls keep him from working with the man he believed was the best publicist in the world.

Mark knew Frishman would be at the 1994 American Booksellers meeting in Washington, DC. Once Mark was there he made it his business to find Frishman and meet in person. Mark knew how he was going to go about this. "You could tell what category someone was in by the color of their badge," Mark recalls. "A person's badge would indicate whether they were, for instance, an author or a publisher. I was looking for the green badge that indicates publicist."

14. Chicken Soup Sales Make History

Suddenly Mark sees the green badge he's looking for. A man is walking toward him and Mark knows from having seen the man's picture that it's Frishman.

"I've been waiting to meet you," Mark says as he goes up to Frishman.

"I know. You're Mark Victor Hansen, the guy whose calls I haven't been taking," Frishman matter-of-factly informed him.

This cold reply didn't slow Mark down. "Jack and I want you to help promote *Chicken Soup for the Soul*. What would it take for you to take us on?"

"Well, for starters you'll need to pay me five grand a month, and you've got to do one media hit a day for the next fifteen years."

To put in perspective the dollar amount that Frishman was asking for, the $5,000 a month in 1994 would mean over $54,000 a month in today's inflation-adjusted dollars. ShadowStats.com says that, for a year in today's dollars, Frishman was asking for $677,000.

That amount may seem enormous but Mark and Jack were all in. They became Frishman's clients. They understood the value of finding the best and paying for it.

From then on, they'd often find themselves flying into a city to do a seminar. They'd finish at 10:00 pm, catch an airplane to their next destination, arrive at 1:00 am, and be up by 3:00 am to do the TV show that Frishman had arranged at 6:00 am. By the third year, Mark estimates that Frishman arranged for them to be on close to a thousand local TV shows.

Mark knew these efforts were paying off because often during a TV show, they'd plug an appearance later that day at a local bookstore. As many as four hundred people would show up during an afternoon appearance. Mark and Jack ended up signing countless books because of these shows.

Speaking of this time in his life, Mark says, "It was exhilarating, exciting, and occasionally exhausting!"

Their original goal had been to sell a million and a half books in a year and a half. As he points out, "We sold 1.3 million books the first year and a half. The second year we sold five million. The third year we sold ten million!"

Meanwhile, Kyle Wilson's friendship with Mark flourished. Wilson remembers that, "At one time he'd call me every day. Within a year, he invited me to be part of the effort, asking me to help write *Chicken Soup for the Entrepreneur's Soul*."

> *"Entrepreneurs have two basic assets: their innovative creativity and their relationships."*
> Mark Victor Hansen

Wilson got to glimpse up close and personal the kind of effort Mark put into building the *Chicken Soup* brand. "Mark would fly into Dallas for an event and have me pick him up from the airport. He would often do a radio interview while still there. He always did at least two radio interviews a day. Back then radio was all-important for selling books. He took the lead in the promotion part of that whole enterprise. I saw how hard he worked at it."

Wilson was fascinated by the collaboration between Jack Canfield and Mark. In his view, they were equal partners. Publishing a collection of inspirational stories was

14. Chicken Soup Sales Make History

Jack's idea, but even so, it was Mark who had encouraged his friend to tell stories from the podium.

In Wilson's view, "Jack was the inside guy working with editors and project managers, and the behind-the-scenes work. Jack was out there speaking as well, but it was Mark who had the bull-in-a-china shop approach to selling and marketing. He was the one who crashed through and made it a success. Jack couldn't have had the Chicken Soup phenomenon without Mark. But it wouldn't have worked for Mark without Jack."

What happened to the partnership that produced a Guinness Book of Worlds Records number of book sales?

You can come across rumors that they had a falling out. Well, it's true that they're no longer close.

I asked Jack about this during a recent phone call. Jack answered, "It wasn't really a falling out. He moved to Arizona so we were no longer geographically close. Also, Mark became involved in entrepreneurial things like investing in energy, while I stayed with writing, speaking, and workshops. That meant we didn't have as much reason to talk every day. We still like each other and every time we talk we have fun. It's sort of like what happens when a neighbor you like moves away."

As for Mark, when he talks about Jack it's clear that he cherishes his time working with his partner. He recognizes that they had complementary skills, and that there's no chance that *Chicken Soup for the Soul* would have been the extraordinary success it became without both members of the team.

Mark and Jack remain friends. Their success turned both men into legends. How did Mark handle the extraordinary success that was coming his way? Did it change him? In the next chapter we'll find out what happened.

Learn from Mark:

- Recognize the importance of promotion. Chicken Soup would have been a total failure if not for the endless slog it took to promote it.
- Be willing to invest money in your success. Hiring publicist Rick Frishman was expensive, but paying for the best was part of the mosaic that made Chicken Soup such a success.
- Understand one of the basic principles of entrepreneurship: fail, fail, fail, fail, fail, fail, fail, fail–and then suddenly, huge success!

15 Mark in His Fifties:
Scaling the Pinnacles of His Professional Life

In his fifties Mark was scaling the heights of professional success. He was widely known as the #1 motivational speaker in the country—he was getting paid $33,000 a talk in this country and in China. He was regularly making $225,000 for three speeches.

In China, Mark and Crystal are the attractor factor before 2016

15. Mark in His Fifties

Along with his partner Jack Canfield, he was also the world's bestselling author. *Chicken Soup for the Soul* sales were making Mark a multi-millionaire. In addition, awards flowed his way: the Horatio Alger Award, the Oprah Winfrey (Oprah's Angel Network), and the Book of the Year Award from the American Booksellers Association, as well as Salesman of the Year Award from Sales and Marketing International.

Mark and Crystal at Horatio Alger Awards, as a recipient, with the American Eagle

Mark's success at this point in his career can be summed up with one word: legendary. What did that kind of success do to him?

Mark's friend, Jerry Silver, an entrepreneur who had known him for a couple of decades by then says, "The remarkable thing about Mark is how genuine he continued to be. He was always the same person on the podium that he is one-on-one. He's also a giver and an egalitarian. He'll talk with anyone who needs help, whether it's the shoeshine guy or a billionaire."

15. Mark in His Fifties

Silver goes on to mention something else special about Mark. "He loves to make fun of himself. He often gave big parties during the period when he was very successful on a national level in marketing and selling vitamins and natural products using multi-level marketing. Mark had a giant screen on a stage, and as the fascinated audience watched, a video of Mark appeared. He was schlepping an extremely large suitcase full of his vitamin products," remembers Silver. "He's having a hard time lugging it up the stairs to someone's house. He rings the bell, a woman answers the bell, Mark starts giving her his pitch, and she turns around and shuts the door in his face!"

Silver remembers that the audience roared. They totally appreciated Mark's self-deprecating humor.

Tip from Your Guide, Mitzi: Self-deprecating humor is enormously attractive. My late husband, Frank Perdue's self-deprecating humor helped propel him from being one of 5,000 chicken growers in Maryland and Delaware, to having a company that today employs 21,000 people and sells all over the world. Frank's TV advertisements made fun of the fact that Frank looked like a chicken and his voice sounded like a chicken squawk . . . and people loved it.

It was during this period that Mark began his professional relationship with Richard Greninger, the audio-visual producer for Mark's events. Greninger was part of the team that helped create Mark's success as a producer of these events. Greninger got to see up close and personal what it took. "Back then we called him the Master Motivator," says

Greninger. "My job included producing large events, four or five per year. We could have 500 to 1,000 people attending. The events would be on, for example, Mega Book Marketing or Mega-Speaking. He was leading people to aspire to their own greatness."

Greninger noticed that were several things that set Mark's events apart from all other contemporaneous events. "He'd always manage to have the best speakers as part of these events. He could do this because he knew everybody of consequence and he knew them well. This meant that he could get the greats such as Harvey McKay (*Swim with the Sharks*), or Dennis Waitley (*The Psychology of Winning*), Ken Blanchard (*The One Minute Manager*), and Art Linkletter (TV shows like *Kids Say the Darndest Things*, *House Party*, and *People Are Funny*.)"

Greninger knows that there was also another factor that set Mark apart. "He really enjoyed the show business side of things. We'd produce amazing shows with videos, a singer, surprise appearances, humor . . . it was show business. He was one of the best at this."

Greninger also got to observe still another side of Mark. "He was exceptionally good at seeing opportunity. His mind is amazing to begin with but he also has a memory that's beyond comprehension. Most of all, he could see clearly.

> *"Opportunity is infinite; once you know that opportunity is omni-existent."*
> Mark Victor Hansen

"The perfect example of this is he figured out how to extend the *Chicken Soup* brand. He reasoned that if there

15. Mark in His Fifties

were a million potential readers who wanted to be writers, he could write *Chicken Soup for the Writer's Soul*. Then he could do the same thing for nursing or basketball or any of a hundred other genres with a million potential readers. He'd find, for example, a famous golfer or nurse, and then work together on a compilation book on golfing or nursing."

With these books, Mark and Jack Canfield had perfected what Mark's friend, the top speaker Dan Kennedy refers to as the "Tom Sawyer, Paint-the Fence" business strategy. This consists of getting others to cheerfully and eagerly do your work for you. People with great stories were eager to have their work appear in the *Chicken Soup* series.

Mark and Jack Canfield in front of Chicken Soup for the Soul wall of fame displaying 254 versions of the book

They'd do the work, and Mark and Canfield would curate the best and have the stories appear in the *Chicken Soup* books. They didn't have to come up with the wonderful stories. There were thousands of individuals who were eager to contribute to the series.

15. Mark in His Fifties

Greninger feels that it's an amazing feat that the *Chicken Soup* series resulted in 254 best sellers that together made over two billion dollars at a retail level, one billion plus in licensing, and a major movie, *Bestseller* with Michael Caine.

Bill Allen is another man who understands some of the reasons for Mark's success. Allen is "The Improvement Specialist." Allen is also an owner of Hawaiian Care and Cleaning with 1,600 employees and inventor of Imop, a company doing over $50 million per year. Mark's relationship with Allen began shortly after 9/11.

"My wife Rebecca will roll her eyes at Mark's exaggerations," Allen begins. "I get why she does this and I sympathize. When I look at Mark, I can see through her eyes that some of the things he says are completely unrealistic. He is sometimes—even often—trying to do things that have never been done before, and he just plain leaves reality behind. He's flying at 30,000 feet and forgets gravity."

But that's not the end of Allen's story. "Even so, and to take Mark's side, when you understand human nature and when you want to create a breakthrough, exaggerating can be an important tool. "Stretching for perfection or a goal that may never happen will take you a lot further than if you're just going for slight improvement. Aiming high, even unrealistically high, can itself be a tool."

That thought leads Allen to an important insight about life and about Mark. "Desire drives ability and will overcome inability. For Mark, that stretching beyond the normal bounds has led to almost incomparable success."

The first time the two men met was shortly after the tumultuous days of 9/11. "When I first saw him, he was in front of maybe eight hundred people at the Jacob Javits

RELENTLESS | 131

15. Mark in His Fifties

Center in New York. The people in his audience had paid $1,000 each to learn how to write a best seller.

"I came with Marshall Thurber and Wally Famous Amos, the promoter of his famous chocolate chip cookies. For the first couple of hours, I was busily taking notes on tools for discovering how to find the best title for a book. Suddenly Mark interrupted his talk to say to his stagehands, 'Get some chairs up on the stage, we've got some additional people for you!'"

"I couldn't believe it. The next thing I hear was Mark Victor Hansen introducing me as the next speaker!" Unexpected as this was, I was delighted to have a chance to present."

Mark and Don King who was a surprise guest at the Book Expo in 2002

There was more to what happened that day. "After I presented, the next thing I knew, there was Don King, the famous boxing promoter who had just had Mohamed Ali doing Rumble in the Jungle fight of his life in Africa. Here was Don King walking down the aisle to meet and thank

15. Mark in His Fifties

Mark for bragging about him earlier to the audience. King was holding high an American flag as the audience cheered."

There's a backstory to that moment. Mark didn't know Don King before that moment but he had watched King on TV the night before and been impressed by King's skill in deflecting the journalistic criticism that was coming his way.

Mark shared with his audience his enthusiasm for King's performance the night before. He told his audience that they needed to be rejection proof, and that Don King was an example of someone who was absolutely rejection proof.

"You will have to be as rejection proof as Don King to become a bestseller at anything," Mark concluded his story. What Mark didn't know at that moment was that King's manager was in the front row listening to Mark talk about King. King's manager called King and told him about Mark's remarks about him. In response, Don came to the Javits Center to show his appreciation to Mark for the story.

That's the backstory of why Don King was walking down the main aisle of the Javits Center to greet Mark Victor Hansen. The flag he was carrying was appropriate given that the event was taking place shortly after 9/11.

Still, Allen was puzzled about just what Don King and patriotic cheering for the flag had to do with learning how to write a best seller. Allen felt this was highly disruptive to those who thought they were there to learn the art and science of writing a mega best seller from the world's all-time expert.

In the end Allen realized that Don King and the flag were a definite plus. "Mark was entertaining the entire room." Allen concluded. "This was an elegant example of 'to educate, entertain!'"

RELENTLESS | **133**

15. Mark in His Fifties

What Allen took away from that day was that people love to be entertained. And Mark's approach meant people became more involved, energized, and receptive. And that above all, edutainment is a surprisingly successful approach. For Allen, "Mark is an edutainer. It's his superpower. With edutainment he unleashes the human spirit. His impact becomes larger than life. It was a huge lesson and a milestone for me on how to present."

Another person who became a big part of Mark's life during this period is Freddie Ravel, founder of Life in Tune™. Ravel is known around the world as the "Keynote Maestro," and he's famous for working with the likes of Deepak Chopra, Madonna, Kanye West, and the teams behind J. Lo, Jimmy Kimmel, and Lady Gaga. He is often referred to as "Grammy-winning piano artistry meets Tony Robbins."

Ravel met Mark at one of Mark's mega marketing book events in 2003. Mark appreciated Ravel's approach of using music to elevate his impact and invited Ravel to come up on stage to present. The two men ended up having a long talk afterward. "The relationship exploded," remembers Ravel, "especially when I learned that he was a musician himself, a bass player. We've been close ever since."

Ravel is particularly aligned with Mark on the notion that, "There is goodness in the hearts of most people. Most of humanity is wired for this. The trouble is the news doesn't show this. What we see on the news tends to be dark."

Ravel sees his friend as coming from the tradition of Napoleon Hill, Dale Carnegie, and above all, Bucky Fuller. They're from the school of American Pragmatism, a tradition that is upbeat and encourages people to be all they can be.

In Ravel's view, much of what we see in the media takes a darker view of humanity. "In the case of the media, the genie's out of the bottle and a lot of the media is dark. It's power for the sake of power as opposed to trying to empower other people for their own good. We're in a narcissistic era, where someone who can write a big enough check can rig the algorithms and use falsehoods to manipulate people's minds."

Continuing in this vein, Ravel observes, "We are living in the Golden Age of Lies, and to counter that, Mark is an ally in the goal for letting honesty and harmony happen, whether in music or in life."

"The most important thing with Mark," emphasizes Ravel, "is he's a beacon of light. He's a champion of great causes, and he possesses fantastic innovative ideation. With Mark, he has so many ideas that it's like popcorn popping. On top of that, his vision is global. Whether it's conservation or technology or the spiritual life, everything interests him."

Ravel concludes with, "I might add, Mark's got Jazz in him. Jazz is about creating ideas on the fly. He does that more than anyone else. Other people get locked in and stick to their knitting. But not Mark. He remains vital and vibrant to innovating what matters most, and I am happy and honored to call him my friend."

By this period in his life Mark was at the top of his game. Many referred to him as the best platform speaker in America. As a speaker and performer he was entertaining, mind-expanding, innovative, and he delivered value. The amazing thing is he experienced a one-in-a-million success with the *Chicken Soup for the Soul* franchise while at the same time being at the pinnacle of the speaking business.

15. Mark in His Fifties

What was left for him?

It turns out, there was a lot.

Sigmund Freud said that happiness is composed of love and work. Mark had the work side of things nailed. The love side? Not so much. In the next chapter, we'll take a look at Mark's failure in this realm.

Learn from Mark:

- See if what's been a success for you can be broadened and stretched. Mark and Jack Canfield parleyed their successful book Chicken Soup for the Soul into 254 additional titles.
- Practice the Tom Sawyer approach of having others do the work of "painting the fence." Position what you want done in such a way that others will want to do it and they'll do it cheerfully and eagerly.
- Aiming high — even unrealistically high — can take you a lot further than if you're aiming for a slight improvement.
- Include showmanship in your presentations. People are more receptive to learning when they're energized with entertainment.
- Don't go after power for yourself. Be a beacon of light that seeks to empower others.

16 A Major Failure:
Mark's First Marriage

Leo Tolstoy famously said at the opening of his 1878 novel *Anna Karenina*, "All happy families resemble one another, but each unhappy family is unhappy in its own way." Happy families enjoy high trust and similar or compatible values. There's mutual respect, they enjoy each other's company, and they're apt to share similar views on spending.

Mark's unsuccessful marriage to his first wife was unhappy and underlining what Tolstoy said, it was unhappy in its own way. However, both partners have been resolutely unwilling to discuss it, and Mark in particular does not want to rake over what went wrong.

This is a classy approach and much to be admired.

However, as Mark's biographer, I have no intention of skipping over one of his greatest failures and sharing it with you. It's one that to this day gnaws at him. It had a major impact on how he treats Crystal Dwyer Hansen, the woman he married in 2011.

Mark's twenty-seven-year marriage to Patty ended in 2005. When he married Crystal Dwyer, it's clear he learned

16. A Major Failure: Mark's First Marriage

at least some lessons from his failed marriage to Patty. Several people who are familiar with both marriages agree that he's doing his best not to repeat the shortcomings and failures on his part that contributed to the first breakdown.

> *"To become enormously successful you will have to encounter and overcome a number of extremely challenging problems."*
> Mark Victor Hansen

Mark met Patty Shaw when he was thirty-one. By most evaluations, he was a rising star. The two fell in love and the marriage produced two daughters. The fact that he couldn't make it last is perhaps his greatest, most tormenting failure.

I've said that neither Mark nor Patty will talk about their marriage. Since they won't talk about this, I've talked with people who observed the marriage from afar. One of these is Mark Wille, a CPA who began working with Mark when he and his then wife Patty were still married.

Wille's point of view is revealing because money can be an x-ray into people's personalities. And in the case of a couple, it can be an x-ray into their relationship. For better or worse money is so personal and so revelatory, that as Wille likes to say, "It can be much easier for a person to be naked in front of their doctor than to be 'financially naked' in front of anyone."

Wille has seen the good, the bad, and the ugly about Mark and finances. He's seen Mark's financial success skyrocket. He also observed the financial missteps and stresses that happened with Mark and his first marriage.

16. A Major Failure: Mark's First Marriage

When analyzing Mark's first marriage, Wille starts by looking at what happened when Mark crossed over from being a well-paid motivational speaker into someone whose books were selling by the millions. Wille got to see Mark go through some of the same problems that, for example a high-paid NFL star or a lottery winner goes through. In Mark's case he transitioned from being a successful speaker, earning what a top-tier speaker was making, to suddenly having an income from speaking and from book sales that was greater than $6,000,000 a year.

That this led to problems isn't entirely surprising. Disagreement on spending, according to a TD Ameritrade report is the final straw in almost half of the divorces in the United States.

Spending habits and diverging financial goals cause stress, and when one spouse makes substantially more money than the other—or even more problematic—if one spouse is the only partner earning money, it can sometimes strain a marriage to the breaking point.

> *"The only people who have no problems, are dead people."*
> Mark Victor Hansen

Wille has seen these kinds of problems many times during his professional career. "Looking at my clients, when I see anyone going from being a regular wage earner to being wealthy, they struggle with the new success and they make mistakes. In Mark's case, some of the spending didn't make sense and didn't match his personality."

16. A Major Failure: Mark's First Marriage

For example, as a CPA who deals with wealthy clients in the Southern California area, Wille has a pretty good fix on what remodeling a house should cost. Wille discovered that what Mark was spending on remodeling his house was much higher than what it cost his other wealthy clients in the same area. Wille doesn't fault Mark for this. In the partnership with his then-wife, Mark's role was earning the money through speaking and book sales. Mark wasn't expecting to take on the bookkeeping role and didn't.

"The bills for the remodeling were two times what they should have been," Wille observes.

Another example of unusual spending that Wille noticed was that Mark and Patty had invested in a house in front of their own home. They rented it out and were getting an attractive cash flow from it. However, as Mark started prospering, Wille noticed that Mark's first wife evicted the renter and used the house for her closet space.

This didn't sit well with Mark. He was brought up to work hard for his money and his family encouraged frugality. While it wasn't a big deal, Wille observed that it was a serious and ongoing irritant.

Patty was beautiful and stylish but Wille noticed there were so many clothes in the supposed-to-be rental property that an outsider might wonder if the clothes would become out of date before they were ever worn. Again, this wasn't the frugal approach to spending that Mark grew up with. His childhood experience of earning the money to buy his own clothes must have influenced his attitude toward what may have felt to him like unnecessarily lavish spending.

The spending wasn't wrong given they could afford it. However, it's an example of what the T.D. Ameritrade

16. A Major Failure: Mark's First Marriage

report was talking about—that differences in approaches to spending, saving, and investing can become the kind of irritant that drives a couple apart.

The situation with clothes and the supposed rental property made Wille think of other newly rich couples who are famous for blowing through millions in a short time. When people suddenly have millions of dollars and don't have a sustainable approach to spending, investing, and creating a lifelong positive and passive cashflow, they soon have nothing left to show for the millions they once had.

That isn't quite what happened between Mark and Patty. Still, the different approaches to spending meant heading in a direction that wasn't bonding as far as the marriage went.

Wille was also aware of another irritant. Patty bought a million-dollar home for her mother on the next street to where Patty and Mark lived. From one point of view this shows Patty in a beautiful light as a caring daughter looking out for her mother. From another point of view it was an irritant because Patty did this without discussing it with her husband. If they had discussed it, Mark might–or might not–have happily agreed to this expenditure and the lifestyle change it created by having his mother-in-law next door. However, the couple didn't discuss this million-dollar decision until it was already made.

By itself, this again isn't a biggie. Mark was traveling continuously. Maybe the opportunity to buy the house meant Patty needed to make a fast decision and there wasn't time to consult him. There could be countless explanations on Patty's side for her buying a house for her mother without consulting her husband. Whatever the truth is behind the decision–and it's unknowable since neither party will

16. A Major Failure: Mark's First Marriage

discuss it–it fits squarely into the category of approaches to financial decisions that can cause stress in a marriage.

Wille was the accountant for Mark and Patty but his life intersected with theirs on another front. Wille lived fairly close to the Hansens. As a hobby, he and his wife enjoyed going to the nearby Saturday garage sales. Patty's spending on clothes ended up being a nice benefit to the Willes.

"Sometimes Patty would have garage sales," Wille reminisces. "My wife and I used to love to go to the ones at the Hansen's. My wife was the same size as Patty and my wife could buy beautiful, expensive clothes that looked like they were never worn. I remember once we bought a gorgeous, barely-worn mink coat which could easily have cost $15,000. We bought it for $30."

These are examples of the spending side of the frictions that Wille noticed. It's not that one approach is right or wrong. But it's certain that when one member of a couple is frugal and one isn't, it opens a wide door to marital stress.

In most marital breakdowns it's rarely one action that becomes responsible for the breakup. It's like the snowflakes building up on a mountain peak in the Alps. The snowpack builds and builds, and then it builds some more. At some point the constant buildup results in an avalanche. But it isn't the last snowflake that causes the avalanche. Rather, it's the ever-increasing build-up that's the real cause of the avalanche.

Those were some of the financial strains, typical of what happens regularly in some marriages.

Mark and Patty had other, probably more serious stressors in their marriage. There were partnership stresses.

16. A Major Failure: Mark's First Marriage

Mark and Patty worked together. In Wille's professional career, he has seen the following pattern emerge many times. One member of the partnership is the creative person and the other is the detail person. The detailed nuts-and-bolts person can become frustrated and even jealous of the attention and the money that flows to the creative person. From what Wille could sense, many of the accolades that came Mark's way as a world-famous author, business leader, and speaker didn't reach Patty.

Wille wonders if Mark and Patty were in the following situation that he has observed with many couples: A wife may feel that she's doing more than half the work and her role is at least as important as what her husband is doing. Yet she is stuck at home doing the behind-the-scenes work which made her husband's glamorous life possible.

Wille observed that Mark was getting 100 percent of the glory, and it was his name that appeared on most of the books and on the awning in front of their office headquarters. As Wille puts it, "In these kinds of situations the behind-the-scenes person may be thinking, 'I'm doing all this work, and what I'm doing is just as important. Why don't I get the fame and glory?'"

When it comes to bestowing rewards, at least in the world we live in today, society almost always provides disproportionate rewards to the creative person. That's not a welcome situation for the behind-the-scenes person who isn't getting the adulation and acclaim. In Wille's estimation, one of the ingredients that prevented Mark's marriage from lasting was the dynamic just described. He thinks a contributing reason for how they saw things differently was, "If you take the optimist-pessimist scale, Mark is redlining

RELENTLESS | 143

16. A Major Failure: Mark's First Marriage

at a ten as an optimist. During the twenty-seven years of their marriage, he was always thinking, 'This was just a bad day. Things are going to get better!'"

This brings up an interesting side of Wille. When it comes to an emotional intelligence quotient, odds are that Wille ranks unusually high. That's in part because, after becoming a CPA, he studied and got a master's degree in theology. When people are talking with him about money problems, he repeatedly finds they talk with him as if he were their pastor or father. This enables him to have greater awareness of what's going on in a marriage than others might have.

Although Wille may have a pastor's sensitivities, there's also a lot of Sherlock Holmes in him as well. CPAs, as part of their professional training, are supposed to be skeptical. Furthermore, they're supposed to use their professional judgment as opposed to taking things at face value.

One consequence of this training was that Wille and Patty didn't see eye-to-eye on some financial transparency issues and she ended up firing him as the couple's CPA. Being fired must, of course, color Wille's view of events, and as the writer of this biography, I'm inviting you to take this into account. Someone who hadn't been fired might take a more understanding and positive view of events.

Although I wasn't able to interview Patty Hansen for this book, she has talked about the ending of the marriage. In an article in the *Orange County Register* she's quoted as saying that Mark told her over a chocolate souffle at the couple's favorite restaurant that he didn't love her anymore and hadn't for a long time.

Patty Hansen later wrote as part of a letter to her children about the divorce, "I wanted to scream 'No! This

144 Mitzi Perdue

can't be happening. Not us! Other people, but not us! Not to me—I am a person who believes true love lasts forever."

However, it didn't. By 2007, Patty's and Mark's twenty-seven-year marriage was over.

They were impressively classy about it. Both Mark and Patty, having personally experienced how shattering and painful this can be, collaborated with Jack Canfield to create a book to help other couples deal with the disappointment, stress, and heartache of divorce.

The result was *Chicken Soup for the Soul: Divorce and Recovery: 101 Stories About Surviving, and Thriving After Divorce*. It was published in 2008, the year after their divorce.

The end of any marriage is complicated. It gets back to Tolstoy and the fact that unhappy marriages are unhappy in their own way. Possibly there's no such thing as a marriage that ends without both being deeply at fault in countless ways.

As we'll see in the next chapter, Mark knows that Patty didn't get the recognition a partner should get. People who watch Mark and his wife Crystal know that he goes way out of his way to make sure that Crystal's role is recognized and celebrated.

Learn from Mark:

- If you're contemplating marriage, make sure you have compatible approached to spending. One of the major irritants that can lead to divorce is differences on attitudes toward money.
- If there's a significant difference in earnings between you and your partner, talk with each other about how you will

deal with this emotionally. If you don't, the situation could breed resentment. Respectfully discuss that either spouse at any time may start to and continue to earn or create more income than the other, and what that might do to the relationship?

- Discuss large financial decisions. Unilaterally making large financial decisions may be justified, but the absence of talking it over and coming to an understanding can create lingering marriage-damaging problems.
- If you or your partner is getting the major accolades and the other is behind-the-scenes, working hard but getting very little of the adulation and acclaim, come to an understanding of how to handle this. One way would be sure to share with the world that the two of you are a partnership and that you recognize and value his or her contribution.

17 Choosing a Spouse: the Second Time

Einstein once said, "If I had an hour to solve a problem, I'd spend fifty-five minutes thinking about the problem, and five minutes thinking about solutions." In his sixties Mark had a big problem to solve, the kind that required a lot of thinking before he could get to a good solution.

By 2005 his twenty-seven-year marriage had ended in failure. The problem he needed to solve was how to avoid making the same mistakes twice. How could he build an intimate, romantic, enduring relationship—the kind he could rely on for stability, security, and joy in his life?

Remembering this period in his life, Mark says, "Most people don't ask questions about what they really want in an intimate relationship. It's too easy, for instance, for a guy to want eye-candy, but there's so much you're missing out on if you stop there. What we really want is to reach the higher levels of the soul, right?"

His approach to solving this problem was to ask himself over a period of months, "What do I really want and need in a relationship?" Ideas began coming to him and he wrote them down as they occurred. The list eventually ballooned

17. Choosing a Spouse: the Second Time

to 267 qualities, values, and characteristic that were for him a must.

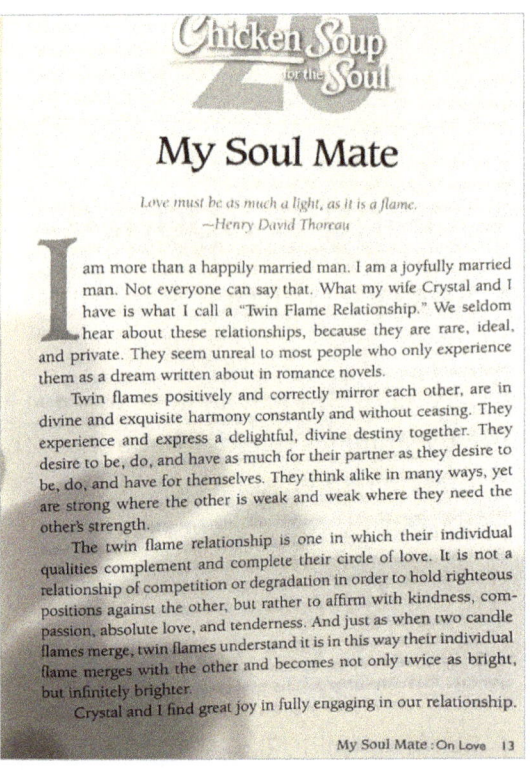

> ### Chicken Soup for the Soul
>
> ### My Soul Mate
>
> *Love must be as much a light, as it is a flame.*
> —Henry David Thoreau
>
> I am more than a happily married man. I am a joyfully married man. Not everyone can say that. What my wife Crystal and I have is what I call a "Twin Flame Relationship." We seldom hear about these relationships, because they are rare, ideal, and private. They seem unreal to most people who only experience them as a dream written about in romance novels.
>
> Twin flames positively and correctly mirror each other, are in divine and exquisite harmony constantly and without ceasing. They experience and express a delightful, divine destiny together. They desire to be, do, and have as much for their partner as they desire to be, do, and have for themselves. They think alike in many ways, yet are strong where the other is weak and weak where they need the other's strength.
>
> The twin flame relationship is one in which their individual qualities complement and complete their circle of love. It is not a relationship of competition or degradation in order to hold righteous positions against the other, but rather to affirm with kindness, compassion, absolute love, and tenderness. And just as when two candle flames merge, twin flames understand it is in this way their individual flame merges with the other and becomes not only twice as bright, but infinitely brighter.
>
> Crystal and I find great joy in fully engaging in our relationship.
>
> My Soul Mate : On Love   13

Mark's written goals about his envisioned soul were published in abbreviated form because of page count.

Here are the first 100 on that list:
1. Available
2. Master kisser/lovingly tactile
3. Similar values
4. Has great personal strength
5. User friendly
6. Elegant
7. Intelligent

148 Mitzi Perdue

17. Choosing a Spouse: the Second Time

8. Conservative personality
9. Great lover
10. Adventure
11. Lives in Southern California or willing to move here if they own another place
12. Well-traveled and willing to travel
13. Totally loves me, and demonstrates it
14. Working on self-mastery and spiritual mastery
15. Likes my business
16. Beautiful and takes care of herself
17. We become each other's number one priority
18. Excited and enthusiastic about life and living
19. Vitally healthy, health oriented
20. Into personal growth and self-development
21. Happy
22. Slender and radiantly fit
23. Has a great personality
24. Superb conversationalist
25. Wise
26. Witty
27. Wonderful
28. Imaginative
29. Magnanimous
30. Philanthropic before I showed up
31. Fun to be with
32. A smile
33. Clean, neat, and smells good naturally
34. Inspires evermore love
35. Cooperative

17. Choosing a Spouse: the Second Time

36. Financially savvy
37. Under-spender- lives below her means
38. Has created some of her own means
39. Knows herself
40. Flexible
41. Social graces and practices
42. Wants us to entertain and be entertaining
43. Playful and adventurous
44. Loves to dance
45. Thinks abundance
46. Wants to create superior memories
47. We can talk forever through the decades
48. Lives in ideas
49. Wants to make the world work
50. Is passionately on purpose
51. Sophisticated
52. We have a profound and growing soulular connection
53. We are soulmates
54. Loves to exercise, stretch, and work on her strength, health, flexibility, aerobics, and balance daily
55. Wants to see the world
56. Nurturing spirit
57. Has deep spiritual practices
58. Meditates
59. Creative
60. Nonsmoker
61. Nonalcoholic
62. Non-drug user

17. Choosing a Spouse: the Second Time

63. Charitable
64. Has great etiquette
65. Is pro-organic foods and healthy eating
66. My friends love and enjoy her personality and are thrilled to be with her
67. Loves my family, kids, and grandkids, and our kids get along—if hers exist
68. Culturally, politically, financially, socially, emotionally, and spiritually aware
69. I can fully feel her love for me
70. Has her own businesses, products, and services to create
71. My staff loves, enjoys, respects, admires, and appreciates her
75. Energetic, and enthusiastic
76. Wholesome
77. Fresh, Spring-like
78. Young-minded, and thinks forever young
79. Neat, clean
80. Original, rich mindset
91. Loves me in all my dimensions
82. Disciplined
83. Not jealous
84. Monogamous
85. Enchanting
86. Seeks out the good
87. Compellingly joyful
88. Sacred experiences
89. Bright-eyed

RELENTLESS | 151

17. Choosing a Spouse: the Second Time

90. Eager to learn forever
91. Wants to serve
92. Positive mental attitude
93. Socially adept
94. Extraordinary
95. Proud to be with me and vice versa
96. Great design sense personally, professionally, for the home's interior, et al
97. Great dresser
98. Beautiful to behold
99. Lives with ease, grace, and spiritual dignity
100. Adoring

Before Mark ever met Crystal Dwyer, the woman he would marry in 2011, he practiced visualization. He was putting into practice the Law of Attraction: that we attract into our lives what we focus on. "In the secret place within my mind," Mark remembers, "I knew she had to exist and be alive somewhere, or I couldn't have had such a clear, purposeful vision of her. I knew she had to be alive and that with every breath I took, I was getting closer and closer."

On May 28, 2008, Mark experienced a stunning example of the Law of Attraction at work. One of the wishes in that long list of wishes was, "I wanted her not just to have radiant beauty. I wanted her to have a radiant soul."

When Mark got up on stage at an Author 101 talk in Los Angeles, he had no idea what was about to happen to him. It was a packed audience, with more than 1,000 people in the room.

17. Choosing a Spouse: the Second Time

As Mark always does before speaking, he looked at his audience, connecting with them, absorbing their energy. As is his way, he privately and quietly recited the Lord's Prayer, invoking wisdom from the Divine Maker of the Universe to give the best talk he had ever given and to help him serve deeply all the attendees.

But this time, as he scanned his audience something unexpected happened. As his eyes were sweeping across the crowded conference room—almost despite himself—they locked onto an amazing vision. What had caught his eye and what had made it impossible to keep scanning was a lovely woman.

There, in the middle of the room, was a vision of loveliness. She was smiling and radiating joy in life.

That beautiful woman was wearing a turquoise top, white pants, and her golden hair seemed to float around her face, framing it and almost glowing like a halo. She was animated, making little graceful gestures with her hands as she . . . oh no! . . . as she talked with the good-looking guy next to her. Mark registered a devastating idea—the beautiful woman was with someone.

Mark delivered his talk, as usual giving it his all. As the professional's professional, he doesn't allow personal feelings to distract him from doing his best with every talk he delivers.

Still, in the back of his mind a painful question nagged. Who was the guy this radiantly beautiful dream woman was with? Was he her husband? Fiancé? Significant other?

He did his best not to keep looking at them. However, in the same way it's hard to keep your tongue from exploring a

17. Choosing a Spouse: the Second Time

chipped tooth, his eyes kept drifting back in their direction. It hurt each time. The glorious blond vision seemed to come right out of his dreams. Yet she might be married or otherwise unavailable.

Mark's talk ended and the woman disappeared but there was a reception that night for those attending the event. Mark found himself surrounded by a dozen or so fans asking for personalized help on how they could write a bestseller. Mark enjoys talking with fans and for him it's a privilege to help them along their road to success. However, in the middle of answering one man's question Mark looked over the man's shoulder and caught sight of the beautiful stranger. She was standing with a group of people across the room.

Mark asked the group surrounding him if anyone knew that woman in the turquoise top across the room, the one with blond hair and wearing white trousers. "Yes," answered one of the people there. "She's Crystal Dwyer, and she's recently divorced."

The knot of pain Mark had been experiencing for hours, the fear that the woman of his dreams might be married, began to dissolve. And the nagging, constricting pain was replaced by hope.

Moments later, as he was watching the beautiful woman from across the room, another woman bumped into her and spilled a full glass of red wine on her white dress pants. As Mark remembers it, "I quickly excused myself from the group, went over to the beautiful stranger, grabbed her hand and said, 'I'm going to take you out of here and get you the club soda we can use to deal with the red wine.'"

17. Choosing a Spouse: the Second Time

They got the club soda; it saved the white pants; and then, as the woman's rescuer, Mark was in the perfect position to invite her for dinner.

"I invited her to the best restaurant in Hollywood," Mark takes up the story. "And there we were having a romantic dinner and she tells me, 'Just so you know, I can't date you. I promised the kids I'm going to spend the summer with them in Idaho.'"

Mark and Crystal didn't date that summer. However, every night they talked by phone for an hour or more. During those conversations, Mark realized that a miracle was occurring. All the qualities he asked for in those visions of his potential soulmate were seemingly manifesting in Crystal Dwyer. He always taught and wrote that you can write down everything you want and it will ultimately, inevitably come to pass. This was a perfect dream come true.

At the end of that summer, Crystal wanted to take an important step in the relationship. They were already dating in person and it was time for Mark to meet her son Weekes. Weekes was twenty-nine-years old at the time and one day, seemingly out of the blue, he got a call from his mom.

"I've got someone I want you to meet," Crystal told her son. "He wants to take us to lunch."

Weekes wasn't feeling enthusiastic about meeting some new man in his mother's life. "I was thinking, 'OK, at least I'm probably going to get a good lunch out of this.'"

It was at the Marriott Hotel in Newport Beach, California. "We get there," Weekes remembers, "and we order steaks. Then I look Mark eye-to-eye, man-to-man, and ask, 'Why do you think you deserve to date my Mom?'"

17. Choosing a Spouse: the Second Time

It was an odd situation given that by this time Mark was world-famous. As Weekes remembers it, "I don't think that Mark was used to having people speak to him like this. Actually, it's not that I think he wasn't used to it; I know he wasn't."

Weekes remembers that Mark seemed knocked off balance. He stammered. In Weekes' view, he was behaving as if it were a job interview, talking about the books he'd sold and the talks he'd given.

But then after the next few minutes the atmosphere changed and Weekes began to feel an emotional closeness to this new person in his mother's life. "After those initial moments, I discovered that he's just a really great person. For the rest of the lunch, I found that this guy who is so famous was the same when he wasn't in the public eye—caring, fun, knowledgeable, wise, and funny. From then on, we've always gotten along well."

A fun sidenote to this. Mark proposed to Crystal over and over again in the two-plus years that followed. "I did this because I enjoyed it so much when she said 'yes,'" he admits.

Mark and Crystal mentioned this funny little routine to their close friend Matthew Ferry, singer, author, and sales trainer. "In response," says Mark, "Ferry wrote a song especially as a gift to us that we gave to everyone at our wedding ceremony and also put it online. You can hear it here: http://markandcrystalsong.com/

Choosing their wedding rings is always an important step in a couple's life. When Mark and Crystal chose their wedding rings, each ring had three diamonds. One diamond

17. Choosing a Spouse: the Second Time

represents Crystal, one represents Mark, and the other represents God. The three diamonds represent a marriage of all three.

The couple married May 8, 2011, in a ceremony attended by 150 of their friends. Among the joyful moments for Mark that day was seeing it was Weekes who walked his mother down the aisle. Mark was so filled with joy and elation that photographs from that day show tears running down his cheeks.

"Crystal is the wisest, most brilliant and radiantly beautiful woman I have ever met. I wrote 267 characteristic, values and virtues of my soul mate and she is 267 out of 267."

"What is wonderful," Mark says of his marriage in the years since, "is we agree on just about everything, and you know it's just beyond astounding how smoothly it's gone."

As an indication of how this continues, here's what Mark wrote in 2020 as a Mother's Day and wedding anniversary tribute to Crystal:

17. Choosing a Spouse: the Second Time

My sparking marital anniversary is my hearts delight.
Because I married my soulmate, and she shines so bright.
She's more than a soulmate—she's my twin flame.
Together, we live life to the fullest, and that's our game.
With her, I am magnificently obsessed.
For my heart, soul, and mind she doth possess.
We do everything together 24/7/365.
We are told we are a formidable couple, and yes, we thrive.
We have written, spoken, and filmed together, and loved every minute.
We subscribe to the theory that love is creativity, and contribution, and so we put all our passion in it.
Combined we have five adult kids and six grandchildren.
And we wouldn't give up any one of them, even for a billion.
Love in our lives overflows.
Everyone remarks and says so.
We are thankful that Crystal's a great and loving mother.
To whom there is no one to compare, in my eyes, not one other.
I love her completely and now you know.
We like, love, and respect one another, and forever this way we will flow.

Your choice of the person you spend your life with—and are closest to—is likely to be the most important decision you'll ever make. When making this choice, copy Einstein and put a lot of thought into the nature of the problem before you make your decision. The best answer will come after soul-searching and becoming conscious of what you want and need in an intimate relationship.

Mark now had the two parts of life in place that Freud says are necessary for happiness, love and work. However, Freud left out something important. It would be really nice if the parents, children, and stepchildren got along. As we'll see in the next chapter, some did and some decidedly did not.

> *"You are here to fulfill your destiny and become all the you that you were meant to be.*
> *Decide I favor of yourself and watch miracles and magic unfold in your life."*
> Mark Victor Hansen

Learn from Mark:

If you'd like to get a jumpstart in romantic success, practice Mark's approach!

- There's a perfect person for you. There are 8 billion people alive today, and absolutely everyone who wants to can find that perfect person.
- Write down what you're looking for. The more clearly you visualize and verbalize in writing what you want and feelingly believe, the easier it is for you to find it.
- Figure out what impact you're supposed to make together. Marriage is about more than romantic feelings. It's about

17. Choosing a Spouse: the Second Time

helping each other to be all you can be, helping you to grow, multiplying your influence for doing good in this world.

- The person should be your force multiplier. As Mark says, "With Crystal, my life has been magnified and multiplied a hundred-fold, or maybe it's a thousand-fold."
- Your marriage partner should be the most important person for you who's living on this Earth.

18 Relationship with Stepchildren and Daughters

Marriage is more than about the couple. It's about the whole family. Mark's failures and successes in this were epic.

Mark's marriage to Crystal seemed made in heaven. Unfortunately a bit of hell can creep into even the best marriages. It happens when a blended family doesn't get along. In the case of a stepson it's a common pattern to harbor deep resentments toward the new stepfather. Or the stepdaughter may deeply resent the new stepmother. Or frankly, anyone can resent anyone.

Crystal's relationship with her two stepdaughters, and for that matter, Mark's relationship with his daughters by his first marriage have not been a success. In this biography, I've tried to give a balanced view, but in describing these relationships there's a roadblock. Mark's daughters declined to be interviewed, and further, I was informed that an invitation for Patty to be interviewed would not be welcome. Neither Mark nor Crystal were willing to discuss it.

18. Relationship with Stepchildren and Daughters

Wounds from decades ago clearly have not healed. To the extent that Mark will talk about the situation he says that he loves his daughters, wishes for a closer relationship, remembers happy times with them when they were children, and is hurt by the estrangement. He wants to fix it but hasn't been able to do so.

On the other hand, Mark's relationship with his stepchildren from Crystal's side seems to be as successful as the relationship with his own daughters has been unsuccessful. It helps that Crystal and her ex-husband navigated their divorce with dignity and respect. Crystal says this helped both of them to remain close to their son and two daughters. "The stepchildren's relationship with Mark has grown stronger through the years," she reports. "The family enjoys spending plenty of time together over family meals, outings, holidays, and vacations."

Her children still enjoy similar activities with their father and his significant other. As Crystal says, "My children, and all parties involved, cheer each other on and advocate for each other. All agree that harmony, kindness, and respect need to be the prevailing attitudes of the whole extended family."

She's noticed her son, Weekes, and Mark have developed a particularly close bond.

As a stepson Weekes could easily have had a painful, strained, and dysfunctional relationship with Mark. After all, fathers and sons frequently have difficult relationships with each other, even under the best of circumstances. A relationship between a stepfather and stepson is likely to be orders of magnitude more difficult.

Weekes and his stepfather Mark are a shining exception. Weekes' relationship with his future stepfather rapidly turned not only into a friendship but a business relationship. "I was running a car dealerships in Utah, and early on Mark became a client," Weekes said. "Our first business transaction was his asking me to buy a car for him. He wanted a newer Lexus, and I helped him trade in his old one."

The business relationship grew. "We started working together in 2016," says Weekes. "Mark wanted to get into renewable energy to carry on Dr. Buckminster Fuller's vision of making the world work for 100 percent of humanity."

> *"We can make the world work for a hundred percent of humanity—for the first time in history—because we have enough of everything, thanks to advancing thinking, technology, the Internet, computerization, and communication."*
> Mark Victor Hansen

As an aside, Weekes points out, "Mark was one of Bucky's best students. Mark worked under him for seven years. Bucky was inspired by Einstein, Mark was inspired by Bucky, and today I'm inspired by Mark. Part of what makes Mark tick is the vision he took from Bucky that "We live on one planet—spaceship Earth—and we need to be more conscientious about how we treat it.'"

Weekes goes on to talk about why Mark founded the solar energy company Metamorphosis and how Weekes ended up working for his father-in-law full time. "I was doing great in my car business, but I liked the idea of a whole other level of interaction with Mark. I left my car business and started working for Mark. It was a fun journey, to see up-close how his mind worked."

Weekes got to watch his father-in-law as a dreamer and visionary. "He's unique," marvels Weekes. "Most of us live in a world of reality but his creativity is unrestrained. My job in working with him was to connect him to the ground. The thing is, 80 percent of his ideas weren't even physically possible, but with 20 percent of them, well, they were something we could work with."

Mark started Metamorphosis from nothing except an idea. "Our approach," says Weekes, "was to create solar energy projects for corporations that hadn't yet adopted solar. We put together turnkey solutions making it easier for them to decide to use solar energy."

"Our first sale was to Chick-fil-A in California, and the second was a Denny's restaurant chain. What made it work is Mark knows everyone. He was the wind beneath the sails, which caused it to work. We started with zero dollars, and three years later, sold it for seven figures. We turned a vision into reality."

Weekes learned something important from this. "The biggest lesson is don't limit your thoughts. Mark wouldn't let anything hold him back. We developed a successful niche in solar because the problem with solar was the ideas were archaic. With fresh thinking, we were providing remarkably effective and innovative approaches."

"For example, we could produce the lowest cost connections by buying factory direct. Small-to-midsize companies couldn't get government grants for solar, but Mark was able to call his friends, and repeatedly, with just a few phone calls, he could solve the financing problem."

18. Relationship with Stepchildren and Daughters

After the sale of Metamorphosis, Weekes went back to his car dealership. Today, however, Weekes is again working with his stepfather, helping him make the **markvictorhansenlibrary.com** a success.

His relationship with his stepfather continues with a closeness that is close to miraculous. As an example, take a look at a letter Weekes wrote to Mark for Father's Day of 2021.

A Father's Day Letter from Weekes to His Stepfather

"Months back we were walking into a business meeting, and you made a comment to me about how you are my 'Business Dad.' That night I got to thinking about it and have wanted to tell you that you are far more than just a Business Dad to me.

"Often we never tell the people around us how really great we think they are. I am not writing this to tell you how great you are, I am writing this to tell you something much bigger. I am writing this to tell you that I love you. Not just a love like you have toward the people you dearly care about, but beyond that. You are so much more than a Business Dad to me.

"You are a Dad to me, and I could never explain through words all that exceptional platform means to me. You are a Dad to me, and you should receive that with the highest honor and importance.

"I love you so much. I love that you take care of my mother with love and compassion. I love that you genuinely play with my kids, care about them, and

18. Relationship with Stepchildren and Daughters

love them. I love that you are a person of deep love, compassion, gratitude, and joy.

"I just really wanted to make sure you know that I could not be happier that God combined you and my mother together, two soulmates, and placed you in my life. I am so thankful for that.

"I want to learn so I can carry that mission on to the world for generations. I want to have my three kids—Everett, Madeline, and Jensen—learn from you to become great leaders, speakers, businesspeople, parents, community members, friends, and philanthropists. I want them to learn from you so they can grow up to live the happiest, best lives possible.

"I love you, and could not let another day go by before I wrote this letter to you so Happy Father's Day, Dad. We honor you today for the loving, caring, giving father you are to us."

Love,

#1 Son

Mark's record in getting along with children and stepchildren is mixed—total failure in part and brilliant success in part. The failure part has gnawed at him for years and although he still holds out hope, even with all his experience, insight, and good will, his current relationship with his two daughters is not a good one. On the other hand, his relationship with his stepson is close and full of love and mutual appreciation.

18. Relationship with Stepchildren and Daughters

Mark and Crystal with his daughter, Melanie Hansen.
She graduated second in class out of 38,000 students at the
University of Southern California

Mark making breakfast with his grand twins, Maddy and Jensen

18. Relationship with Stepchildren and Daughters

In Mark's relationships with his children and stepchildren, he hasn't batted 1000. However, he has an impressive record in nourishing friendships, as we'll see in the next chapter.

Learn from Mark:

- With relationships, you can't expect to bat a thousand. Mark may be one of the most gifted people alive when it comes to maintaining successful relationships. Even he couldn't navigate a supportive and loving relationship with his ex-wife or their daughters.
- With respect, trust, and good will, a blended family can work. Mark gets along well with Crystal's children and grandchildren.
- If you have an entrepreneurial idea, learn from Mark's approach. In the case of the solar energy company Metamorphosis, Mark proved he could create a company that can be sold for seven figures starting with nothing more than an idea. But in addition to vision, it also takes work, contacts, financing, and generally being all-in.
- Don't limit your thoughts. What enabled Mark to build a company in a sector that was already mature was because he was so innovative that even though only twenty out of a hundred ideas would work, those twenty put him ahead of his competition.

19 By Helping Friends Mark Continues to Touch Lives

I have a theory of life, one that you'll see more than once in this book: Success is measured not by what you can get, but by what you can give. It goes along with something Aristotle said 2,300 years ago, "The only way to achieve true success is to express yourself completely in service to society."

Mark's track record of being able to give to others puts him in the one-in-a-million category. Come with me and take a look at some of the individual lives he's touched. Here are some quick stories of how Mark inspired:

- Jim Stovall, a blind man to make $100 million dollars in the movie industry;
- Jim Karoll, the world's greatest mentalist, to expand his professional work;
- Carlton Pearson, a bishop, to recover from the worst time in his life, and then extend and broaden his spiritual understanding and influence;
- Zoe Hazan, a college student, to explore and expand what her future could be;
- William "Pila" Chiles to go from "lost, and rudderless" to having faith and direction in his life.

19. Touching Lives

Jim Stovall, Blind Author, Movie Maker

Take first the case of Jim Stovall, author, movie maker, and multi-millionaire entrepreneur. Stovall is in the unusual situation of not being able to read the bestselling books he's authored. Likewise, he's unable to view the popular movies he's made. Stovall lost his sight in 1958 when he was just twenty-one years old.

Mark was responsible for this sightless person's career in moviemaking. If you were to talk with Stovall about how this happened he would quickly tell you, "My movie-making career began because I asked Mark to write an endorsement for my book, *The Ultimate Gift*."

Stovall didn't know Mark, but it's common for authors to ask famous people for endorsements. Keep in mind that the odds of a positive response are small, especially when the author is as famous as Mark. In fact, Mark gets so many requests for book blurbs that he's said, "If I answered all the requests I get, I'd be writing endorsements all day long, and wouldn't have time for doing anything else."

Stovall's request was the exception to Mark's policy of not writing book endorsements. To Stovall's astonishment, Mark didn't just write a blurb for *The Ultimate Gift*. He also wrote as part of the endorsement, "I see this as being one of the all-time great movies!"

As Stovall tells it, "No one else had thought of this. Because of Mark, the book became the basis for a trilogy of movies that have grossed over $100 million. I don't think anyone would have paid attention to me if Mark hadn't got people thinking about the movie potential. His words in the book endorsement opened doors in the movie industry."

Stovall says of Mark, "He is the most giving guy I know. Here he had this amazing vision of what I, a blind guy, could be and the funny thing is, he had to convince me that my book could be a movie before he convinced Hollywood. He has the vision to see you being better than you ever imagined and then he does the things to get you there."

Stovall goes on to say, "He gives of himself to other people for no reason other than to help. He reached out and changed my world for the better. The truth is I got rich and famous trying to catch up with Mark's vision for me. It was a case of one plus one equals 100."

By the way, if you want to see *The Ultimate Gift*, you can rent it on Amazon, and here's an inside baseball tip for when you watch it. The producers from FOX invited Stovall to have a cameo appearance. "I'll play anything but a blind guy," he told them. They cast him, a blind guy, as the limo driver who interacts with the main character.

Mark helped Stovall with his $100 million career in the movie industry. Interestingly, Mark's contacts also helped another friend with his career Jim Karol.

Jim Karol and Deception Detection

Jim Karol got to know Mark because Karol's friend, former Director of the Selective Service System, Bill Chatfield called him one day saying, "Jimmy I got somebody you have to talk with." Karol was surprised to discover that the "somebody," was the *Chicken Soup for the Soul* guy, Mark Victor Hansen.

Karol experienced what many others have—Mark is as personable on the phone as he is on stage or in person. "Mark turned out to be the nicest guy in the world," marvels

19. Touching Lives

Karol. "We bonded instantly on the phone and we still talk frequently. We'll get into conversations on a huge range of topics, whether politics, the unknown, or dreams. We really bonded over the dream I had that I died and then woke up and heard voices feeling euphoric. We talked about this maybe twenty times."

Mark has continually put Karol in touch with people who can foster his career as a performer. Karol marvels how often Mark has gone out of his way to share his Rolodex to benefit his friend.

For those who know Mark, it's no surprise that he would find his new friend fascinating. Karol is known as the "World's Greatest Mentalist," and among his achievements, if you tell him your town he can almost certainly tell you your zip code. That's because Karol has memorized more than 80,000 zip codes. If you're mathematically inclined, you may know that the mathematical function Pi is 3.14. Memorizing Pi to two decimal places wasn't enough for Karol. He's memorized Pi to thousands of digits.

Karol reports that Mark is particularly interested in a specialty Karol has developed—deception detection. That is, how do you tell if someone is lying or telling the truth? Karol has made a science of this. He now works with the Department of Defense, sharing his special skills. This new assignment came about in an odd way. He was sitting at a poker table at Las Vegas. Across the table from him was a two-star general, General Ashley. Karol demonstrated to the General that he could tell every time when the General was, for instance, saying falsely what suit a card was.

In other words, Karol could know when a general was being deceptive. After a few minutes of this a guy taps Karol on the shoulder and says, "Sir, do you know who that is?"

"Sure, he's General Ashley."

"No, do you know who he really is?"

Karol shook his head.

"He's Lieutenant General Robert P. Ashley, Jr., Director of the Defense Intelligence Agency. He's military intelligence. He's the top guy!"

Karol was in Las Vegas to entertain participants at the Warrior Games, but as a result of his interaction with General Ashely, Karol ended up working for the Department of Defense, helping the US military with his almost supernatural skills at deception detection.

Karol also knows almost everything you could imagine about body language, tone of voice, eye dilation, and other "tells" about when someone is not being straightforward. It's interesting to see how a man with these skills judges Mark.

Karol says, "He won me over with one conversation. I think the world of him, and I can't think of anything bad to say about him. Everyone has a fault, but I don't know what his fault is."

Remember, these words were spoken by a guy who knows more about reading people than almost anyone else on the planet!

Bishop Carlton Pearson and Grow with the Flow

Bishop Carlton Pearson met Mark during the lowest point in his life. A little more than twenty years ago, Pearson

19. Touching Lives

was known as one of the most beloved Pentecostal Christian personalities of his generation. Thousands would fill arenas and churches to hear him sing, preach, and inspire.

Things turned upside down when Bishop Pearson began to preach a more inclusive approach to spirituality. His message was about interfaith dialogue and fellowship while rejecting spiritual bigotry.

It didn't go over well.

Seemingly overnight, one of the church's most beloved members went from hero to zero. Pearson had the horrifying experience of being labeled the "most prominent heretic of his generation." In the process he lost his influence, his church, his friends, and seemingly, the ability to make a living in his chosen field.

It was at this point in his life that he met Mark. Bishop Pearson knew that Reverend Ike had been a huge inspiration to Mark during the lowest time in Mark's life. Looking back on this period in his own life, Bishop Pearson says that Mark provided the same kind of inspiration for him that Reverend Ike provided Mark.

Bishop Pearson remembers the moment when they first met. Pearson's friend Bishop E. Bernard Jordan introduced Pearson to Mark, and to this day Pearson remembers, "Mark's huge smile, his warm physical embrace, his loud and reassuring voice. We've since become fast friends. He's literally been chicken soup or as they say the 'Jewish penicillin' for my soul!"

Encouraged by Mark, Pearson was able to see that life's breakdowns can be turned into breakthroughs.

"Experience is not only what happens to us but what we do with what happens to us," Pearson says. "The point isn't to go with the flow but to grow with the flow, even when it becomes a flood."

Mark's lessons of hope and love and growth didn't only help Pearson, he rescued Pearson's friend from despair. As Pearson tells it, "A businessman friend of mine who'd just filled Chapter 11 flew with me to one of Mark's book seminars out West. We'd both just experienced the worst professional losses on our lives."

Pearson introduced the man to Mark. Continuing the story, Pearson says, "Mark gave him the kind of healing embrace, both physically and spiritually that instantly gave my friend an amazing sense of hope, of being helped, and of happiness that he hadn't received in a while. For whatever reason, Mark, out of the clear blue, presented my friend to the crowded conference which led to my friend's getting a book deal."

Pearson goes on to say, "Because of his interaction with Mark, my friend regained his self, his soul, his zest for life." Pearson adds, "He had the same impact on my life." Pearson feels that somehow Mark "never meets a stranger."

In Pearson's view that's one of Mark's best traits. It's true whether Mark is one-on-one or with a large audience. "He somehow reads and relates to any room he's in regardless of its size or structure. Even his name reflects that. His name "Mark" is the Greek word scopos from which we get out English word scope—perspective or vision.

Pearson has seen that Mark loves to help the underdog or people who are hurting, struggling, or in any way marginalized. He loves to see others recover and succeed.

19. Touching Lives

Mark is good at this, Pearson believes because, "He's known both lack and abundance. He's gone from living in his car to helping people buy them."

"He's a man for all seasons," Pearson summarizes. "He's a rare specimen of the best of human light, love, and excellence. He helped gently guide me out of traditional religious limitations and bigotry into new thought, expanded consciousness, and introduced me to an entirely new world of friends and associates. He helped change my life dramatically. I'll always feel eternally grateful both to and for him."

So, what became of Pearson, after becoming friends with Mark? Today, his life story serves as the basis for the Netflix original titled Come Sunday. It highlights his personal story about the shift in his ministry to radical inclusion, insisting that Christians are not the only people who will experience eternal life. The movie premiered at the Sundance Film Festival in January, 2018.

Zoe Hazan, a College Student Finds Herself

Mark has impacted the famous and wildly influential but he also influences young people who are finding their way. Zoe Hazan is one.

In September 2020, college-age Zoe Hazan just didn't seem to know what she wanted to do with her life. Further, since this was the height of COVID-19 pandemic and much of the country was on lockdown, there didn't seem to be a way for her to get the job experience that could help her figure things out. She felt at sea.

19. Touching Lives

Somers White, the famous speaker, is a mentor to Zoe and he suggested she apply for an internship with Mark Victor Hansen.

Here's what Zoe Hazan says happened next. "I drafted an email with the help of Somers, asking Mr. Hansen if there was anything a University of California, Santa Cruz undergraduate, could help him with even though it would be remote work and at the height of the pandemic."

For Hazan, this felt like a long shot. However, Mark is about helping people, and he agreed. Of course, it also helped that Mark has close-to-infinite respect for his friend Somers White and would naturally be inclined to say "yes" to any request that originated with White.

Mark's agreeing to hire the young college student turned out to be an important break for her. He was working on marketing his new book ASK! and since this was a time of COVID, Mark's usual approach of speaking to conventions of thousands of people just wasn't on the table.

Mark gave Hazan the assignment of getting him invitations to be on podcasts. In case you're not familiar with podcasting, a podcast is like a radio or television broadcast, except you can access it on the Internet. Podcasts are typically hosted by an individual or individuals who lead a conversation, share stories, or report the news. By 2020 it was possibly the best medium for selling books.

The assignment Mark gave young Hazan was a game-changer for her. "When I first started I barely knew anything about the world of podcasting," she admits, "but I gave it a shot."

She turned out to be good at it. She researched which podcasters were accepting guests and which might be likely targets for her efforts. Soon this twenty-one-year-old undergraduate was proving herself by getting bookings for her boss. She'd cold-call major podcasters and get Mark booked, and sometimes she was able to arrange for as many as five guest appearances in a day. For the young woman, it was a tremendous confidence-builder.

Mark gave her assignments that provided her a sense of accomplishment and pride. Her proud father acknowledges that this was life-changing. As Zoe Hazan says, "I think Mark was impressed. At the beginning, he didn't know if I could deliver, but in the end he let me know I had proved myself."

In the time since, Hazan has graduated. As of 2022 she has the self-confidence she didn't have before. She knows that she can deliver. She's learned that she loves working with people, loves reading, loves writing, and she is excited about using her degree in film and legal studies. She's found herself.

William "Pila" Chiles, from Rudderless to Purposefulness

William "Pila" Chiles describes himself as a "trainer in neurolinguistic programming." Today, he's a Fortune 500 speaker who's taught on the "Whole Life, New Age" lecture circuit for twenty-seven years.

He's also a former homeless veteran whose life Mark turned completely around.

They first met in 1984 at one of Mark's Sunday morning church sermons in Kona, on the big island of Hawaii. It was during a period when Chiles considered organized religion to be nothing more than hypocritical, shallow, outdated nonsense.

Pila only went to the service because a friend of his, sensing that Chiles was "lost and rudderless," insisted that he attend. Pila's problem was severe Post Traumatic Stress Disorder (PTSD), the result not only from being wounded in combat in Vietnam but also from having his Marine combat unit suffer some of the highest casualties of the war.

Meeting Mark became a pivotal moment in Pila's life. He went from feeling lost to having direction and faith. His feelings toward organized religion have changed from feeling that church is archaic and obsolete to "coming back to the church."

The fact is, Mark's sermon changed everything. As Chiles tells us, "I was so moved, I walked up to Mark Victor afterward and placed my most valued possession on his head. It was a Panama hat with a beautiful purple feather lei, and then I simply turned and walked out."

Under normal circumstances, that should have been the end of it. And yet, somehow Mark understood this wasn't just some eccentric stranger doing something decidedly weird. After all, putting a hat on Mark's head, without even explaining why would, to most people, appear strange.

Not to Mark.

Mark took the trouble to track down the phone number of Pila's Kona art gallery and bookstore and called Pila from the airport. You might expect the phone call should have been the end of things. After all, it could have been a nice, short chat with Mark thanking Pila for the hat and that would be it.

However, that's when the coincidences began. Pila lived just ten minutes from the airport, and a friend came into his store at just the moment while Pila was on the phone.

19. Touching Lives

Without hesitation the friend did two things that enabled Pila to drop everything and drive to the airport to meet Mark. The friend, a former minister himself, agreed first to watch Pila's store for him and second, to let Pila borrow his Jeep to drive to the airport. As Chiles sped off to the airport another coincidence happened; Mark's plane was delayed.

That meant time to talk. As Pila remembers it, "We partook of the 'elixir of the gods' (Kona coffee) . . . and chatted about the world's problems 'until our hair caught fire.'"

And what happened as a result?

Chiles' life has turned around. He's gone from being a homeless veteran who was overwhelmed by PTSD to being a man who speaks to Fortune 500 organizations. Today he inspires others.

Something else Chiles values that came from that first meeting with Mark. As mentioned earlier, Chiles had no use for organized religion. Today his attitude is, "In this critical, defining moment, and turning point for humanity, we must come back to the church and its umbrella of God's love if we are to survive. And, as the church teaches, when love permeates all, life is no longer just about survival."

Chiles' final assessment of Mark is, "He can inspire a marble statue, move mountains, and have you in tears of laughter at your best friend's funeral. That's only the tip of the Mark Victor Hansen's 'iceberg.' It can sink the Titanic of fear while dispelling all doubt. It is my observation and conclusion over many years, that Mark's 'superpower' lies somewhere between government-level diplomacy and the Apostle Paul's ability to raise the dead."

19. Touching Lives

Mark was now by almost any measure an outstanding, maybe one in-a-million success. Was he ready to rest on his laurels? Or maybe, was he destined to be like the champion boxer, who's reached the pinnacle of success and then gets overtaken by competitors? And then keeps trying again and again for the comeback that never comes? The next chapter has answers.

Learn from Mark:

- You never know how a small act of kindness can change a life. In the case of Jim Stovall, Mark's endorsement made a $100 million difference in a man's life.
- Having an open and friendly personality can mean exciting friendships. And it can also mean access to exciting knowledge, such as in the case of Jim Karol, and learning to tell when someone is being deceptive.
- Have the attitude Mark taught Bishop Pearson—life's breakdowns can lead to life's breakthroughs.
- Don't go with the flow. Grow with the flow!
- Help young people with their self-confidence. Making it possible for a young person to earn their self-confidence can change the trajectory of their lives.

20 His Sixties: What Does a Man Like Mark Do for an Encore?

By the time Mark was in his sixties, the two parts of life that Freud says are essential for happiness—namely love and work—were well in place. The part that was a gaping hole in his life—a close, intimate, and loving relationship—was finally filled. His relationship with Crystal is the kind that his friend, the late Bob Proctor, describes as, "The best thing that ever happened. She's a beautiful person; she's so good to him; she loves him; she is forever wanting to do things for him. He hadn't experienced this before. She's endlessly kind and sensitive to him simply because that's the way she is. You could write a book about how to treat people if you followed her. He is so happy today. He's really enjoying his life."

Proctor knew Mark since the 1970s, and saw him through a twenty-seven-year unfulfilling marriage. The love side of Mark's life was now in better shape than it had ever been. What about the work side for a man who was already at the top of the ladder, whether as a speaker or author? What new heights were there to scale?

A short answer to what Mark did for an encore is, more of the same.

In 2008, the founders of the *Chicken Soup for the Soul* series, Mark and Jack Canfield, sold a major stake in the company to a new ownership group led by Bill Rouhana and Bob Jacobs. The sale was for $63 million.

This meant a change in Mark's and Jack's relationship with their original publisher HCI. As Peter Vegsos tells it, he was originally expecting to be their publisher for life. At one point in the discussions, there was an issue of who owned the trademark "*Chicken Soup for the Soul.*"

Vegsos felt that usually the publisher would own the trademark but Mark's first wife Patty Hansen told him, "We want to leave that to our kids." Vegsos felt that since he expected to have the publishing contract for life it wasn't that important to him, and besides, "Emotionally I was on their side about leaving it to their kids."

In Vegsos' view, this turned out to be a major mistake. When Mark and Jack sold the publishing rights to Rouhana and Jacobs, the trademark went with it. That meant the new owners would be publishing the *Chicken Soup* books. Vegsos felt he had been thrown under the bus. "It was a lousy ending to a great story," Vegsos summarizes.

New ownership of the *Chicken Soup* series was soon to result in big changes. Until 2008 *Chicken Soup for the Soul* had been mainly a bookselling business. Books were ninety percent of the profits of the company. But the firm had already begun to diversify the brand into dog food.

When Rouhana and Jacobs bought the trademark, they saw the broader potential of using the brand for products in adjacent fields. By some calculations, the profits from licensing the *Chicken Soup for the Soul* brand resulted in a 10,000 percent growth in revenue in just three years.

20. His Sixties: What's Next

Rouhana and Jacobs were able to successfully extend the *Chicken Soup for the Soul* brand because of the brand's meaning of hope, faith, and trust. According to one Harris poll, eighty-seven percent of people in the US have heard of *Chicken Soup for the Soul,* and almost everyone who hears the name has a feel for what the brand symbolizes.

The short answer to the question of what would Mark do after so much success was truthfully "more of the same." However, he wasn't destined to share the sad fate of a champion boxer who has his big win and then never makes it again, vainly hoping for the comeback that never comes.

Mark was, and is, the extreme opposite. His friend Mark Fournier is an EMMY Award-Winning filmmaker, author, keynote speaker, and coach. Fournier sees Mark as, "The quintessential model of someone living life to its absolute fullest and continually striving to realize his full potential."

Fournier believes that Mark's greatest asset is a limitless mindset. "It's like Elon Musk; everything is possible. As the adage goes 'What man can conceive and believe, he can achieve.' This simple axiom has been around for so long that it's easy to dismiss, but it doesn't make it any less true—especially if you're Mark Victor Hansen!"

Fournier compares what Mark does to what President Kennedy did back on May 25, 1961. Kennedy announced back then that we would land a man on the moon by the end of the decade and then bring him back safely. Fournier explains that many brilliant and knowledgeable scientists had warned Kennedy not to make that promise. The technology, they informed him, just wasn't there. However, Fournier states, "The power of Kennedy's belief brought this accomplishment into existence. Once people accepted the goal, they reverse-engineered it into being."

> *"Goals have a tendency to be realized all at once. So, set too many goals and keep adding more goals."*
> Mark Victor Hansen

In Fournier's view, "Mark does this reverse engineering better than anyone else I've ever met. The inevitable obstacles are for him just speed bumps. For him, it's boom! The universe opens up."

When asked about Mark's failures, such as bankruptcy and divorce, Fournier challenges, "Failures? What failures? My definition of a failure is the absence of growth. The price of this growth may be very painful, but each one of his setbacks have shaped him into what he is today."

Fournier adds, "If any of us knew ahead of time how painful some of these learnings can be, we'd probably run away from them and hide. We'd refuse them no matter how much we'd learn. We'd answer, 'No it's too painful; it would be like sticking a fork in my eye.' So, the universe gives us a nudge when it comes to the lessons we need but aren't quite ready to take on."

Reflecting on his friends financial and relationship setbacks, some of which were truly painful, Fournier believes that every one of them had value for Mark. "They've given him insight and understanding about what others are going through or will go through. I can't call them failures because he learned from them all."

20. His Sixties: What's Next

All of this fits in with Fournier's favorite quote by George Bernard Shaw. "Life isn't about finding yourself; it's about creating yourself."

When looking at Mark's life, Fournier concludes, "One of the greatest things we can ever aspire to is in knowing that when we've left this planet, we've done the best we could to leave this world a little better than the one in which we were born—that we have left our mark.

When it comes to Mark, he will most surely have left his 'Mark' both literally and figuratively—in fact, his impact will have been so great that when Mark is gone from this planet, he won't have just 'put a dent in the universe' as Steve Jobs aspired to; he will have kicked a hole in it!

One of the examples where Mark "kicked a hole in the universe" had to do helping special needs children in Mexico. We'll find out about it as we explore Mark's fifty-year friendship with the Lehrers.

> *"Goals are for a lifetime. They are voluntary, yet a mandatory assignment—if you want to be someone, who does something, and has something— set and get great goals."*
> Mark Victor Hansen

Learn from Mark:

- Having scaled one professional peak doesn't mean resting on your oars. Keep on, working at your highest and best level.
- Keep striving to reach your full potential.
- Will your success into being. Failures aren't failures if you learn from them, and they form the basis for future success.
- Failure increases your ability to understand your fellow man.
- Make your legacy leaving the planet the better for your having lived on it.

21 A Fifty-Year Friendship, the Lehrers

Lindell and Steve Lehrer have been friends for five decades. They met in the early 1970s at an International Yoga Conference. "We just hit it off," remembers Lindell. "It was that magical feeling you get when you know someone is going to be important to you for a long time."

This was back in the time when Mark was living in Long Island, trying to sell Buckminster Fuller's geodesic domes. "The three of us were fans of Napoleon Hill's *Think, and Grow Rich*," remembers Lindell. "We were into Mastermind groups and self-improvement." Back then, notes Lindell, "Mark was driving an old, beat-up Volkswagen, and he was so into the idea of geodesic domes that he even had one on his bed."

> "All advancement, all success, all achievement starts with thinking, personal relationships (best called Master Mind Relationships), innovation, creativity, and self-initiative-to-action"
> Mark Victor Hansen

21. A Fifty-Year Friendship

Commenting on this, Mark says, "I actually had an eight-foot in diameter, three-quarter dome with a door opening to crawl into my bed. Probably the only one like it. Its novelty attracted a lot of attention from visitors."

Those were the early years. By 1974, Mark's speaking business was taking off, and Lindell and Steve were starting their business of buying and fixing up homes in dilapidated areas. They bought one home for two thousand dollars, fixed it up, and flipped it to Mark for fourteen thousand dollars with a two thousand dollar down payment. Three years later they sold Mark's fixer-upper for a walloping fifty-eight thousand dollars.

Once during this period when Mark accidentally double-booked a speaking engagement, he asked Lindell if she would cover for him and give a talk to the local Rotary. The local Rotary had offered Mark $25 for the talk. Mark told her, "I'll give you my $25 if you'll speak there instead of me." Lindell agreed to help out her friend.

The weather the night of the Rotary dinner was nasty. It wasn't just cold. It was snowing and blustery. Lindell would have far preferred to stay inside in her cozy home. Still, she got her act together, showed up, and covered for Mark.

You would think that this is a simple story with no need for further information. However, there's something seriously (well not really seriously) wrong with this picture. Mark never got around to paying Lindell the $25.

"I remind him about the $25 every time I see him," says Lindell. In the forty-two years since, compounding interest of six percent, Mark owes Lindell $289. However, if we use ShadowStats.com for this calculation, what he really owes her, taking inflation into account, and the fact that 1980

RELENTLESS | 189

21. A Fifty-Year Friendship

dollars were worth more than 2022 dollars, the amount is closer to $3,000.

The $3000 debt that Mark "owes" Lindell dwindles in size, compared to what she owes him. Here's why everything more than balances out.

Today she and her husband support a school in Mexico for the disabled. "In 2007, we had one of the worst hurricanes ever in Mexico. In a short period of time, we had sixty inches of rain."

The school they were supporting suddenly couldn't pay the light or the phone bills, and the school was about to go under. Frantically, Lindell called her pal Mark.

"How can I save the school?" she wailed.

On the other end of the line, Lindell heard Mark answering her question with a question, "What can I do?"

Lindell asked if he'd be part of a $150 a plate fund-raising dinner for what is affectionately called "The Little Yellow School House." Mark agreed without hesitation. He came to Isle Mujeres, Mexico, off the coast of Cancun.

With Mark as a speaker and because of his efforts in alerting people to the importance of the event, the Lehrers raised an almost unthinkable $12,000 for the school. "That $12,000 not only got us out of the hole," says an awed Lindell, "it meant we could build a kitchen so the students could learn cooking skills which would mean secure jobs for them in the hospitality industry."

21. A Fifty-Year Friendship

Mark and Crystal with Americans living in Isla Mujeres, Mexico, talking and helping raise money for the Little Yellow School House for at-risk and special needs kids

With the momentum from the initial fundraising effort that Mark helped spearhead, the school has since benefited from a fundraising music festival and yearly fishing tournaments. By 2022, the school had nine classrooms and sixty-three children in the school.

Each year, the students are blessed with the chance to learn skills that will help them hold good jobs and have the pride that comes with being contributing members of society. Lindell feels that Mark's willingness to give of himself made much of this possible. "The depth to which he has touched these young lives is almost unfathomable."

The Lehrers were delighted when Crystal came into Mark's life. Their friendship with Mark had lapsed during his twenty-seven-year marriage to Patty but it came roaring back when Crystal entered the picture.

21. A Fifty-Year Friendship

"When we first met Crystal they were not yet married, but we knew instantly that she was the one," remembers Lindell.

Looking back on their four decades of friendship, Lindell Lehrer says, "He has a gigantic view of life. We knew him from way back when he was just starting, a man who was driving a broken-down old Volkswagen. Still, he was a man with dreams of becoming a best-selling author."

"The impressive thing is, he did it. Through force of personality and understanding of how the world works, he made his dream come true. His great gift is his ability to conjure up for other people the feeling that they too can make it."

Lehrer feels that in Mark's life, "He's been very consistent, and it's proven out that when you encourage people to think bigger and to think above and beyond, they can maximize the gifts they've been given, and go beyond what they ever expected. What Mark preaches works."

One of the things Mark teaches is tithing. In the next chapter, let's take a look at how this has worked for him and how it can work for you.

Learn from Mark:

- Think big, maybe even think the impossible. When Mark was in his 20s, he dreamed of becoming a bestselling author, and with that focus in mind, thinking made it happen.
- Be a force multiplier for others. Because Mark helped the Lehrers with their fundraising, hundreds of special needs children learned the cooking skills that guaranteed them well-paying jobs.

22 Tithing, a Bedrock Principle that Guides Mark's Life

One of the bedrock principles that guided Mark's life is the necessity and the privilege of giving back. When he looks on his lifetime of faithful tithing, he sees it as both a cause and an effect of the enormous success that has come his way.

To most of us, tithing is giving away ten percent of our earnings. It may seem daunting and impoverishing. But Mark's life experience demonstrates the opposite. He discovered this important principle. "Giving does not cause you to have less. No. It guarantees that ultimately and inevitably you'll have more."

Mark has seen in his own life that as he tithed he became more successful. That meant that the amount he was able to tithe kept increasing. As the amounts he tithed grew, his success also kept skyrocketing. This giving and then receiving and then giving more has been, for Mark, a miraculous virtuous circle.

The mainspring of his desire to give is spiritual. A large component of this is gratitude. When he thinks about tithing

22. Tithing, a Bedrock Principle

he realizes, "Everything we have is a gift from God. The air we breathe, the water we drink, the mind we think with, the world we enjoy, absolutely everything. God created it, and proudly said 'All that I have is yours . . . '"

How could one not be grateful?

Mark continues, "Einstein said the universe 'is finite and boundless.' When you contemplate the vastness of the universe or even the smallness of our planet Earth with a diameter of eight thousand miles and a circumference of 25,000 miles, you have to think, 'Wow, and it's all mine to experience—and enjoy!'"

He likes to quote Genesis 1:26/7: " . . . *we are created in the image, and likeness of God.*" He draws from this the understanding that, "We are stewards of the Earth, our lives, and our destiny."

In his book, *The Miracle of Tithing*, he explains what he calls the four Ts of tithing. He believes that we are here to give back 10 percent of our:

- Thinking
- Time
- Talent
- Treasure

The bonus T is: Thankfulness.

Mark firmly believes, "You have more to give than you can even start to imagine. Give and you will have more to give. Treat yourself and your world that way with total thankfulness of heart, soul, mind, and body."

What about where your tithing should go?

He answers, "This can be to your church. Or it could be charities that you like, trust, believe in, and that are doing

22. Tithing, a Bedrock Principle

great and honest work, and their administrative costs are below 10 percent."

Mark sees tithing or giving as being like water—it comes in three forms. He puts it this way:

- When you don't give, your life is frozen and hard and breakable, like ice.
- When you give a little, your life flows some like warm water.
- When you tithe proportionately, ten percent, as requested in every spiritual system, your life becomes like a vaporized drop of water expanding everywhere.

Mark feels that once you experience being like vapor with goodness expanding everywhere and feel the miracles happening in your life, you will never stop giving. "Givers gain and non-givers feel pain," he says.

Mark goes on to say, "In my experience, abundance seems to be underwritten by contribution. The oldest spiritual literature on the planet is the Upanishads, the opening line of which says, 'Out of abundance, He or She took abundance, and only abundance remained.' There is more than enough for everyone everywhere."

He feels his whole life has been continuously teaching him this lesson of abundance and giving back. When he was a student ambassador to India, he went to Mahatma Gandhi's home, and one of his affirmations on the wall said, "We have enough for everyone's needs, but not for anyone's greed."

Mark lives what he preaches. "Given my philosophy, I have tithed to a different charity on every book that I have

22. Tithing, a Bedrock Principle

ever written. I am frequently asked why I have sold more books, according to the Guinness Book of World Records—over 500,000,000—than anyone else alive. I answer, 'It is because I am a constant giver.'"

Currently, Mark, and his wife Crystal are helping the Horatio Alger Association for Distinguished Americans where the association has funded over 35,000 scholarships to college or technical school for at-risk deserving kids.

"I can tell you that miracles are spontaneously happening in our lives because we are givers. I recommend you choose to test out the above thinking and see if you don't get an enormous never-ending payback."

Mark has given away millions of dollars as he tithed, and he's tithed in other ways. In the next chapter, we'll take a look at other efforts at making the world a better place.

Learn from Mark:

- To jumpstart your life of success and abundance, practice tithing.
- Take advantage of the principle of abundance. The way giving works is, it accelerates the process for ultimately having more.
- Create a virtuous circle in your own life. As you achieve more success, you'll have more to give.
- Give back as an expression of gratitude. Being grateful for all that God has given us is one of the secrets of happiness. True gratitude is shown with acts.
- Check out Mark's book, The Miracle of Tithing. You can find it on amazon.com or on his website markvictorhansen.com.

23 Mark and Childhelp

When Mark works for a charity, he brings to bear the same kind of energy and focus that he does with everything he touches. Founders of Childhelp the world's largest nonprofit dedicated to helping victims of child abuse, Sara O'Meara and Yvonne Fedderson have experienced Mark's caring and action firsthand.

Mark and Crystal, Co-Chairs of Childhelp Fund Raising Campaign with Sara O'Meara and Yvonne Fedderson, Founders

"We met forty years ago," says O'Meara. "We were both living in California and we had two reasons to meet. First,

23. Childhelp

he was extremely interested in our mission of supporting children who needed help. Second, I have the gift of healing, and at the time, his child was in the hospital seriously ill."

We'll get to what Mark does for Childhelp in a moment, but first, what about his ill child?

Mark, frantic with concern for his daughter, begged, "Sara, your prayers are so powerful. Please pray for my child. She's in ICU, she needs your prayers."

O'Meara prayed for Elisabeth, and a seeming miracle happened. Elisabeth hadn't been doing well and her doctors feared the worst. But then, coinciding with O'Meara's prayers, Elisabeth began to get better. Her color improved. Her breathing improved. To her worried father, it looked as if she was coming back to life.

In the forty years since, Mark has been a continuous supporter of Childhelp. "The side that I know of him," says O'Meara, "is something I know more deeply than most, and that's his spiritual side. He is a very kind, warm-hearted person, always willing to help and to lift people up."

She gives as a quick example of how Mark interacted with her grandson John Charles Hopkins. At the time her grandson was the student body president at Arizona State University. He was attending a church service where Mark was present. The student was way younger than Mark, and it would have been easy for him, as someone who's world-famous to pay no attention to the boy. Still, according to O'Meara that's not what happened. Mark focused his entire attention on the young man and seemed to enter into his world and his way of looking at things. Mark would ask questions and then listen—listen—listen.

23. Childhelp

O'Meara watched Mark make her grandson feel important and valued. Mark was looking at the young man's face, enveloping him in the cone of his attention, shutting out the hustle and bustle of what was going on around them, revealing how deeply interested Mark was in every word the young man was saying.

O'Meara saw firsthand that Mark clearly wanted to know what was going on in the young man's life and what if felt like to be a part of this younger generation. O'Meara was in awe over how skillfully, yet naturally, Mark was able to draw the young man out.

In O'Meara's view, "This was an example of something Mark does that counts for a lot. When he's in a conversation with you, he's truly listening to you. By focusing on you, and nothing else, he's communicating to you how important you are to him. It's not just at a social level. No, it's at a soul level. You feel it and see it."

She has an opinion on what motivates him to make people feel important. "It's his heart that motivates him. He has a beautiful heart. He's deeply caring about people. It's always about the other person as I saw when he was talking with my grandson."

We've just been talking about the more spiritual and human side of how Mark has interacted with people at Childhelp, but his contributions have also been much more concrete. O'Meara is impressed by how often he's made book donations to the children at Childhelp. Sometimes these donations have been gifts of five hundred books at a time.

The books are exactly on target for the children at Childhelp. *Chicken Soup for the Teenage Soul: Stories of*

23. Childhelp

Life, Love, and Learning has been particularly helpful, but other books have been important, such as the one for *Chicken Soup for the Preteen Soul: Stories of Changes, Choices and Growing Up for Kids Ages 9-13*. "The books are very inspirational because they have terrific messages for children. They're especially great for reaching teenagers," says O'Meara. In O'Meara's view, these inspirational books have made a huge difference for some of the eleven million young people her organization has served.

Mark's benefit to Childhelp didn't stop with the tangible gift of books. He also understands that an organization like Childhelp needs money. He always tithes royalties he's received from his books, and many times, Childhelp has been the recipient. These are substantial amounts of money.

But his contributions to Childhelp go beyond money and books. As O'Meara points out, "He and Crystal use those connections to open doors for us in Washington. With his help we've gotten child advocacy bills passed in Congress. He is willing to share his connections. He has many friends in all walks of life, and he doesn't mind asking his friends to help others."

Yvonne Fedderson, the other founder of Childhelp, share's O'Meara's appreciation for Mark. "We're all given talents in life but many times we don't use our gifts or talents to the fullest. Mark does, and then, as he's prospered himself he used what he's gained to help others."

Fedderson has a final thought on Mark. "He's sincere. Sometimes people say and do things for ulterior motives, but what Mark does, he does from the heart. God needs people like him. He and Crystal are good examples. God needs us to keep our lights shining even though some days it's kind of hard."

We need examples because they help inspire us to help each other, and life is about helping each other. Read on because the next chapter has other examples of how Mark was able to help others.

Dr. Frank Lutz's home where a simulated White House was a backdrop for a Childhelp Charity event that Mark made happen

Learn from Mark:

- Hone your listening skills. Through listening you have the ability to make people feel valued and important. You can change their image of themselves.
- Share your connections. You may not be able to help get bills passed in Congress the way Mark does, but you almost certainly know people who can help other people.
- Be an example. As Fedderson says, "We need examples because examples help inspire us to help each other, and life is about helping each other."

24 Mark and Teaching Others to Give

Mark, and Jack Canfield sold the trademark for *Chicken Soup for the Soul* in 2008. They made $63 million from this deal, but Mark wasn't one to rest on his laurels.

He was already on the radar of Tom F. Painter, the entrepreneur and "compassionate capitalist." What Painter may be most famous for is his work as co-founder with Robert Allen of the Enlightened Wealth Institute. Painter's life intersected with Mark's when Mark's book *One Minute Millionaire* began selling millions of copies and creating countless millionaires in the process.

However, creating millionaires runs up against two conflicting approaches to thinking about making money. The Scriptures admonish us, "Don't let your left hand know what your right hand is doing." But Scriptures also say, "Let your light so shine before men, that they may see your good works, and glorify your Father which is in heaven."

As Painter sees it, "Mark had a tremendous influence in making it okay for people to talk about making money." It helped that Mark also was an example of tithing.

As Painter sees it, Mark is clearly on the "Let your light so shine" side of things. Mark began working with Painter

24. Teaching Others to Give

on the Success and Money Foundation. He donated time and money to help create some of the three hundred free online courses available at **successandmoneyfoundation.org**.

The Success and Money Foundation teaches kids, teens, young adults, and adults about learning to earn and earning to give. "We have more than three hundred free online courses based on the success and money secrets from people like Mitzi Perdue, John Paul DeJoria, Peter Thiel, Elon Musk, Jeff Bezos, and Robert Kiyosaki," points out Painter.

The kids who've learned financial literacy and then made money through the online courses are taught the value of giving back. They get to choose what they support and what they're passionate about. "We even have a leaderboard and the competition for donating is a wonderful force."

"Something special about Mark," adds Painter, "a lot of people talk, but Mark makes things happen." One of the ways Mark made things happen is using *Chicken Soup* royalties to help with Painter's free education effort.

Painter sums up his view of Mark saying, "He makes a difference and whether you're a waiter or the President of the United States, he wants what's best for you and your family."

Brad Rotter, a large-scale investor who helped pioneer financial futures, came into Mark's life in 2018. Like Painter, Rotter values giving back. Rotter is a self-described "impact" investor and in his case impacting is about strengthening the security of the homeland. His focus has been on cybersecurity.

Rotter's knowledge of cybersecurity led him to a deep understanding of bitcoin. He sees the societal value of digital money that's instant, private, and free from bank fees. As he puts it, he's ". . . been breathing the blockchain ever since."

Brad first met Mark Victor on a due diligence call in 2018. Mark served as chairman of the board of **naturalpowerconcepts.com** in Oahu, Hawaii. Natural Power was exploring the use of energy from ocean waves to produce cheap, renewable, carbon-free energy. The people on the phone call were using their personal expertise to evaluate the company's commercial potential.

There were eight people on the phone, but in just a couple of minutes Rotter realized that one person on the call stood out. The person was breathtakingly bright and exceptionally visionary. It was Mark Victor Hansen.

Rotter didn't invest in the company, but he did end up becoming friends with Mark. Today they're on the phone with each other almost weekly, bouncing ideas off each other, whether on philosophy, economics, investments, geopolitics, or the future of the Republic. If ever there's a case of "It takes one to know one," it's Rotter recognizing Mark as an extremely intelligent man and a visionary leader.

Rotter, while still a young man, co-founded the Chicago Finance Forum in 1984. Members included economists, industrialists, traders, and business executives. Since then, they've been meeting monthly to discuss what was going on in their respective verticals. Like Mark, Rotter enjoys looking at the world through a wide lens, and he's turned on by the ever-expanding benefits that can come from technology.

Today, Rotter's professional passion is to accelerate the union of quantum information science, blockchain, and artificial intelligence. "The blockchain and digital currency

24. Teaching Others to Give

thing is way bigger than the Internet. It is the internet of value. Most important, it is happening at a much faster pace than the Internet did."

Although Mark and Rotter are each clearly one in 500,000 when it comes to intelligence, that's not their biggest bond. It's revealing that Rotter's involvement in Mark's world is philanthropy.

"Mark introduced me to Childhelp. It's the biggest organization working to prevent child abuse," says Rotter. "Mark gives Childhelp part of the royalties from his books. I know about this because one day he called me up and said, "Hey, Rotter, I want you to come to an event at the home of Frank Luntz, the pollster guy. It's a fundraiser."

Rotter brought twelve people to the event, and has been heavily involved in supporting Childhelp ever since. Mark and Crystal were the co-chairs of the fundraiser.

Mark initially bonded with his friend Brad Rotter because they are both smart. But today, the bond is more than just a bond from the head. Even more, it's a bond from the heart.

So far we've been talking about giving time or money or insight. In the next chapter, we're going to be talking about shedding blood for charity. It's taking philanthropy to a different level, but it's one that people can do no matter how much money they have or don't have.

Learn from Mark:

- It's more than okay to make money, but giving away substantial parts of it is an inspiration to others and agrees with the scriptural guidance about letting your light shine so as to glorify your Creator.
- Learn to earn so that you can give benefits to everyone.
- Philanthropy is a powerful bond to grow a friendship. A bond between two minds is a great thing. A bond between two hearts is even greater.

25 Mark and the Nation's Blood Supply

When Mark supports a charity, he's all in. His efforts during the 1990s helped prevent a crisis in the American Red Cross blood supplies. Today, he's addressing a similar blood supply crisis. Oh, and here's a spoiler—what you're about to read is going to involve you.

From 1991 to 1999, his friend Elizabeth Dole was President of the American Red Cross. In the middle of her term she found herself up against a severe problem—the American Red Cross faced a shortfall in blood donations. She telephoned her longtime friend Mark Victor Hansen.

"Can you help?" she asked urgently. "We need more donations. The need is critical."

Mark wasn't about to turn down his friend. "When do you need it," Mark asked.

"Yesterday!" Dole answered.

"Let's go to the medical doctors," Mark suggested. "They can help."

"We've already tapped them. They're great, but it's not enough. We're almost out. This is close to desperate!"

Mark was ready to help. He was one hundred percent on board with the importance of donating blood while encouraging others to do so as well. It was a role he was familiar with since the time when he was a teenager.

We'll get to what he did for his friend Elizabeth Dole and the American Red Cross in a moment, but first, a flashback into why Mark was so receptive to Dole's request.

It started when he was sixteen years old. One life-changing day, Mark got an urgent phone call from Bailey, his oldest brother. Bailey's best friend was in a serious car accident, and before the ambulance could get him to the hospital the young man had lost so much blood the situation was life-threatening. Bailey appealed to Mark to donate blood immediately. "My friend will die without blood donations," Bailey frantically told Mark.

Mark swung into action and was able to do more than donate just one pint of blood. When he got the call from his brother, Mark's rock band, the Messengers, were in the middle of a practice session for that night's concert.

Mark takes up the story, "The five of us dropped what we were doing and went to the American Red Cross Blood Bank to donate. Then that night, while we were giving a rock concert in Waukegan, Illinois, we invited everyone in the audience—and there were hundreds of them—to join us in volunteering to give blood. We learned later that because of that plea, many others also went to the Blood Bank and donated."

Jump now from 1964 when Mark first got involved with donating blood to the mid-1990s, when Mrs. Dole asked Mark to help. This coincided with when Mark had just attended a service at Dr. Robert Schuller's Crystal Cathedral in Garden Grove, California.

25. The Nation's Blood Supply

Mark with Dr. Robert Schuller, host of Sunday Hour of Power telecast to ten million viewers

Because of his teenage experience, Mark was already on board with the importance of blood donation, but Dr. Schuller told a heart-wrenching story that strengthened Mark's commitment. Dr. Schuller's daughter Carole Schuller was riding her motorcycle in Iowa when a speeding truck whisked by the young girl, catching her left leg in the well of one of the truck's wheels. Carole's leg was instantly ripped off, and she was thrown bleeding into the ditch. By the time she was rushed to the nearest hospital, she had lost so much blood she was close to death. Multiple transfusions saved Carole's life. Dr. Schuller faced the terrifying knowledge that if lifesaving blood hadn't been available when his daughter was brought into the hospital barely alive, she would have died. Dr. Schuller knew his daughter lived only because others had given blood. From then on, he asked his congregants to give blood at least once a year for the rest of their lives.

And now, back to Mark's 1990s conversations with Elizabeth Dole. Realizing that the Red Cross needed a new approach, Mark suggested that her organization enlist a source they hadn't used before, the nation's 77,000 chiropractors. "I've spoken at their conventions, their universities, and their professional improvement meetings for years—they almost all know me," Mark explained to Dole. "They're great people. Combined, they see twenty-five million patients a month, and I think they'd be eager to help, and not only that, I bet they'll do it cheerfully!"

Mark has a long-term relationship with the nation's chiropractors. In fact, in the view of Dr. Sherry McAllister, President of the Foundation for Chiropractic Progress, it's not just a relationship. It's an emotional connection. As McAllister puts it, "When Mark speaks, he'll often share with the chiropractors what was the low point of his life, going through bankruptcy and having only a few dollars in his pockets. He'll take his audience through the worst part of his life, and show them how he came out the other side. They could feel how Mark managed to have the resilience to get beyond abject failure. In McAllister's view, Mark was good at lifting everyone's spirits and giving them not just hope but proven tools for success.

Given that Mark had a close relationship with the whole profession, and given that he admires their low-tech, drug-free, high-touch, cost-effective, holistic approach, Mark was in a great position to ask the leadership of the chiropractic community for a favor. He explained the urgency of donating blood and then he asked if they would help with an American Red Cross Blood drive.

There was more to it than just asking if the chiropractors would donate blood. Mark figured out how to benefit not

25. The Nation's Blood Supply

only the American Red Cross and the individuals it serves but the community the chiropractors serve.

This being prior to the Internet, he suggested that the chiropractors mail letters to all their inactive patients offering them a complimentary adjustment if they'd donate blood. As an added bonus, Mark donated a nicely bound booklet with three chapters form his latest book, *A Third Helping of Chicken Soup for the Soul*.

The booklets cost his publisher, his partner Jack Canfield, and himself $.25 each. They ended up giving out a million and a half copies. Anyone who donated blood could get one of these, and between an adjustment and a complimentary excerpt from one of the world's most popular books, Mark was able to inspire so many blood donations that the American Red Cross was able to freeze enough blood to meet their needs for almost a year and a half.

Meanwhile, the chiropractors were back in touch with their inactive patients, to the great benefit of their communities' health and the chiropractors as well.

That's what happened almost thirty years ago.

In the years since, Mark has remained a staunch advocate of the American Red Cross and blood donation. The way he looks at it, donating is a selfless act that takes less than thirty minutes. However, he knows that there are enormous personal benefits for you the donor, going even beyond the satisfaction of knowing that your action saves lives. Again Mark comments, "Any donation of blood is a big positive karma. In virtually all faith traditions, sowing means a future of reaping."

Fast forward to today. The American Red Cross is again in critical need of blood. Because of the pandemic and lockdowns, many businesses, colleges, and universities were forced to skip their usual blood drives.

In too many areas, instead of the usual five to seven days of blood supply, the local Blood Banks' available blood has dwindled to only one day's supply. In some hospitals, surgeries are postponed until the blood supply is more secure. When there's a car accident or a particularly tough childbirth, an individual may not survive without a transfusion.

Today Mark is again helping with an American Red Cross Blood Drive, but before I share with you more information about it, it's time for a full disclosure. In the other cases of Mark's philanthropic activities, my job as his biographer, is to record and to observe what he's done and is doing.

This case is different.

I'm personally involved with this activity, and my dearest wish is that you would also feel personally involved. Mark is helping with a blood drive where people are invited to go to their local American Red Cross Blood Bank to donate. Or they can join a blood drive.

Join Mark in the Relentless Blood Drive. If you're in the United States, you can learn where the nearest Red Cross donation center is if you'll go to:

https://www.redcrossblood.org/give.html/find-drive

Once you're there, the website will let you know the nearest Red Cross donation center or where there will be upcoming blood drives. You'll also have a place to sign up for a blood donation appointment. The whole process is seamless and convenient, and I know this because I've done

25. The Nation's Blood Supply

it.

When you've signed up, the Red Cross will send me a notice that you've done this, and I'll make sure Mark Victor Hansen sees that you did it! The Red Cross will be tracking all the donations that come about because of this book. Let's make Mark proud, while at the same time doing something important and life-saving.

I'm so looking forward to hearing from you! And even more, I'm eager to show Mark that you heard the call.

Mark with some of his books

"It's not that people want too much, it's that they want too little and get it."
Mark Victor Hansen

Why does Mark give so much to efforts like the Red Cross blood drive? In the next chapter, we'll have a look at more about what makes him tick.

Learn from Mark:

- Donate blood. According to the American Red Cross, one blood donation will save at least one life and often more.
- Knowing you've saved a life can give you a super great feeling. It's a for-sure self-esteem booster.
- And, when you've donated blood, send me a selfie of you doing it, and I'll make sure you get a copy of the *Fable of Micaela*.

26 Other Friends Talk About Mark

In this chapter, let's take a look at a personal aspect of Mark. We'll be seeing:
- How Mark helped a guy with a medical issue
- Why Mark is good at inspiring everyday people
- When Mark gets taken advantage of
- Whether Mark has a vindictive, litigious side to him

Jerry Silver and a Medical Issue

"One of the defining characteristics of Mark is, he cares for people," begins businessman, attorney, and entrepreneur Jerry Silver. "As an example, here's something having to do with a medical issue that only a really caring person would do."

"One day Mark calls me, asking, 'Jerry, how're you doing?'"

"Not so good. I've got diverticulitis. I'm having an operation in three weeks, and they're taking out a foot of my intestine."

"Don't you dare do that," the voice on the other end of the line ordered, adding urgently, "You have to see Dr. Mick

26. Other Friends Talk About Mark

Hall first. He has extraordinary healing techniques that go way beyond the normal procedures in medicine."

Before talking with Mark, it had never occurred to Silver that he could avoid surgery. Diverticulitis is a painful condition of the colon, and he knew he absolutely had to do something about the debilitating pain. Surgery to end this horrible pain seemed the only answer.

Mark set Silver up with a doctor's appointment for 10:00 am a couple of days later.

Silver showed up at the address Mark gave him. However, meeting with Dr. Mick was unsettling for Silver. Dr. Mick wasn't giving off the vibe of being a typical doctor.

"Are you a medical doctor?" a nervous Silver asked.

"I'm a naturopath," the man answered.

Silver bristled with skepticism. The skepticism was understandable given that part of Silver's career was in developing medical devices, and he knew many respected medical doctors throughout the country. The environment he was in right now wasn't what Silver was used to.

However, as he quickly learned, Dr. Mick's approach was that he wasn't there to treat symptoms by cutting out a foot of Silver's intestine. Instead, he was there to discover the underlying causes of Silver's illness and address those.

Dr. Mick explained to Silver that an alternative to undergoing surgery was changing his diet. Dr. Mick prescribed for him natural products high in fiber and also recommended specific stretching and strengthening exercises.

Silver was approaching all of this with something close to total suspicion. To his surprise, over the next few days he began seeing that Dr. Mick's recommendations worked.

"Within three weeks, my diverticulitis was gone," marvels Silver.

Silver was spared the pain, expense, and anxiety of major surgery. To this day he continues to use some of the same protocols and products for prevention.

Mark had cared enough to go out on a limb recommending non-traditional medicine for his friend. Mark had actually gone to the trouble of making the appointment.

Jeffrey Hayzlett and Mark's Reaction to People Taking Advantage

Jeffrey Hayzlett, as a business celebrity and as a renowned speaker, frequently runs into Mark at corporate events. They've been friends since the 1990s, when *Chicken Soup* was at its height. Part of their friendship is based on their ability to energize each other.

"When the two of us get together, it's like nuclear reactor rods being pulled out of the cooling tanks," says Hayzlett. "It's pure energy! But something else I get to see that the public doesn't is his love of his family, his love of life, his constant efforts at self-improvement, and his endless desire to help others. He's a Tasmanian Devil in a Scandinavian body."

> *"When you improve, the whole world improves."*
> Mark Victor Hansen

Hayzlett and Mark don't share the same political views, but interestingly, that's never interfered with their friendship. They both can respectfully explore each other's strongly held opinions while staying close friends.

They may be good friends, but that doesn't stop Hayzlett from observing that Mark has a problem with trust. Hayzlett echoes what Mark's accountant, Mark Wille says, "If I were to name Mark's major flaw in life, it's that he's too trusting." Hayzlett sees this plays out with Mark's being vulnerable to being taken advantage of. He sees Mark as someone whom others want to use for his fame or money or contacts.

Hayzlett was fascinated by how Mark reacted to cases where he's seen people take advantage of him. "He's never acted vindictive or uttered a foul word about these people," says Hayzlett. That's Hayzlett's view.

Kyle Wilson and Mark's Being Litigious

There are others who would disagree with Hayzlett. They see Mark as being litigious.

Kyle Wilson, for instance, dropped his friendship with Mark for years because he saw Mark as being too ready to involve lawyers when there was a dispute. Also, there's the fact that even though Mark's and Patty's divorce was publicly classy, they were in court three times after the divorce.

My own view is that Mark has a litigious side to him. From the way he conducts himself, I think the story he carries inside his head is something along the lines of, "I'm one of the nicest guys you'll ever meet, but don't try to take advantage of me."

I believe this is one of the internal stories that guides Mark's life. In the next chapter we'll take a deeper dive into the power of stories to shape us.

26. Other Friends Talk About Mark

Learn from Mark:

- You can demonstrate true friendship by going out of your way for a friend. Mark actually set up a doctor's appointment for his friend Jerry Silver.
- If you are having trouble with diverticulitis, check into whether a diet high in fiber might be beneficial for you. What's right for one person may not be right for another, but it did help one of Mark's friends.
- If a lot of success or fame comes your way, there will be individuals who will want to take advantage of you. Brace for this, and figure out how you will handle being a target for such people.
- Think ahead of time how litigious you want to be. It's a choice. I can see the utility of settling nuisance lawsuits and going to extremes to avoid them in the first place. On the other hand, I know people who will fight any time they're sued as opposed to settling. They take this approach believing that not doing so would encourage other shakedown artists.

27 Ken Walls:
Proof of the Power of Stories

Want an example of the power of Mark's stories? Look no further than Ken Walls.

Ken Walls is one of the world's more popular podcasters. His show "Breakthrough Walls" has a listenership in the millions and he's an Amazon Influencer.

His life wasn't always like this. Before the *Chicken Soup* books came into his life, Walls was an alcoholic from a broken home and as he put it, "This was my life, and this was the way it was going to be. I'm going to die a poor and broken person."

He never went to college. As he tells his story, "I grew up in an incredibly poor family. My father ran off when I was two years old, and my mother then married a monster who made my life hell complete with horrific beatings."

Like others who never receive a vision of a better life, Walls might have just settled for continuing on the dismal path heading to nowhere.

Things changed when he came across the *Chicken Soup for the Soul* books. "I began to see possibilities. I decided I wasn't going to let myself be a victim of being poor, " he says.

27. Ken Walls: Proof of the Power of Stories

"Since reading *Chicken Soup for the Soul*, I've read many of Mark's books, some of them multiple times. I know I've read *The Aladdin Factor* four times. It was *The Aladdin Factor* that made me feel that there's hope for my life. I don't know anyone who is better at delivering a message of hope than Mark. What humanity needs more than anything else is to know that's there's a greater purpose to life."

Walls began aiming for bigger and better things. As he takes up the story, "I put in the work to become a better human and then set out on a mission to help others do the same. It is now my mission to help others have their breakthrough. You can overcome trauma, loss, addiction, a failing business, and hardships, yet find joy, confidence, recovery, and success. I have done it and you can, too."

With this kind of message, his career as a podcaster grew and grew. Then one day, something amazing happened to him. It was in the year 2021. "I got a voicemail related to my podcast. I remember walking out of my office and having my wife listen to the voicemail just to make sure it was real. It felt like having the King of England call me."

The voice recording was from Mark Victor Hansen asking about being on his podcast. When Walls had that first actual phone conversation with Mark, he told him, "I can't even believe I'm on the phone with you."

Why?" the voice on the other end of the line said. It was warm, non-threatening, curious, and most of all, it sounded as if the person was someone who cared.

"I'm a college dropout," blurted out Walls.

"No problem, it doesn't matter what you didn't do, and it doesn't matter what you did wrong. It's tomorrow that counts. It matters most what you really want to be and do from now on."

During that first conversation Walls got to tell Mark something that was on his mind, namely, how much Mark's books had impacted his life and in such a positive way. In the years since, they've talked frequently and Walls always leaves those conversations feeling inspired—one of the reasons Walls feels uplifted after talking to Mark. "A lot of people are out for themselves. They're asking themselves, 'What's in it for me?' Mark has always struck me as someone who's question is 'What's in it for everyone?'"

Our next chapter is going to be about something that can be beneficial for everyone.

Learn from Mark:

- Change your life by changing your story. Ken Walls feels he might have had an unsuccessful life, dying poor, and broken. Reading the *Aladdin Factor* gave him a better vision of what he could be. By changing his story to one of possibility and hope, he took the steps to become a fuller, bigger person. Today he's one of the world's more popular podcasters.

- It doesn't matter what you did wrong or what you didn't do. It's tomorrow that counts! It matters that you have thought through and written down in detail what you want to be, do, have, and what your destiny of choice is."

- Develop an authentic interest in the well-being and growth of others. Part of Mark's success is that he's not asking, "What's in it for me?" but rather, "What's in it for everyone?"

28 The Power of Stories:
How They Can Change Your Life

Have you heard the phrase, "We are the stories we tell ourselves?" Basically, Mark teaches that we shape ourselves through stories. The good news is, with the stories we tell ourselves, we can re-invent ourselves and become new and better versions of ourselves.

Mark has seen that stories are like little computer programs inside our heads, guiding our actions and telling us how to think about things. For shaping who we are and how we act, nothing is more important than stories—nothing!

It begins in childhood. Some memory researchers believe that our earliest memories go back to two and a half years old, although that may be the outer limit. More likely your memories won't go back quite that far, but often your earliest memories set the stage for who you are and what you become. And the glorious thing is by writing about them you have the power to edit them.

Let's take a quick look at how this has played out in Mark's life. His story is an example of the power stories can have in guiding and forming our lives.

28. Stories Can Change Your Life

Mark's earliest memory, described in the first chapter, is of his mother telling people that she had the best boys on the block. This story influenced his identity the rest of his life. He wanted to live up to what his mother thought of him.

Stories from throughout Mark's life influenced him. In his twenties Mark experienced, in the most painful way, what negative stories can do to you. His initial story was he got to study with the great Buckminster Fuller and was going to build geodesic domes to provide affordable, easily constructed housing for all of humanity. He was king of the roost. He was a genuine hot shot!

That story served him well until the Oil Embargo in 1973. When the Organization of Petroleum Exporting Countries (OPEC) embargoed oil shipments to the United States, manufacturers could no longer make the petroleum-based polyvinyl pipes Mark needed for his geodesic domes. He couldn't fulfill his contracts and in a matter of weeks, he lost an almost incredible $2 million. At twenty-six he was bankrupt.

"I've lost everything," Mark was telling himself. "I've failed."

The story he was telling himself got worse. "It's not just that I failed. I myself am a failure!"

He became depressed. He kept thinking of the dreams that would never come true and the people he had let down, and the promises he had been unable to fulfill. The negative story he was telling himself didn't stop there. Broke, despondent, sleeping on the floor in a house with four roommates, the stories he was telling himself turned

RELENTLESS | 225

28. Stories Can Change Your Life

dire. Unable to sleep, tossing and turning on the hard floor, he even told himself, "I'm such a failure that I don't want to live. Maybe I should kill myself."

In the early hours of one sleepless, tormented night, a desperate Mark asked God what he should do. The answer he received changed his story instantly. His conversation with God allowed him to know with certainty that his destiny was to be a speaker.

Hearing God's answer changed his internal story from, "I've failed so badly that I don't want to live," to "My destiny is to be a professional speaker and writer!"

Shortly after this, by what must have been divine intervention, Mark heard a man who helped Mark grow and enlarge this story about his destiny. Reverend Ike taught Mark the story he has lived by ever since—everything is possible and he should imagine himself fulfilling his destiny. The destiny was to use speaking and writing to inspire people and to help them have better, fuller, more satisfying lives. With this new story guiding him, Mark took on the daunting task of becoming a professional speaker. And stories of encouragement helped him become a success.

The power of stories accompanied him for the rest of his professional career. His success came not only from the stories he told himself but also the stories he shared with others. His speaking career focused on telling upbeat, redemptive stories. These helped people view life through a new lens; the lens of hope and the knowledge that adversity could be overcome.

This formula of telling redemptive stories helped inspire his audiences to (metaphorically speaking) rewrite their own stories. Members of his audiences could reframe their lives seeing themselves not as failures, but as powerful, energetic winners who could prevail against the odds.

Soon Mark was telling these stories in speeches around the world. Audiences of thousands would come to hear these stories of redemption and triumph over adversity. These stories led him and his colleague Jack Canfield and to write the *Chicken Soup for the Soul* series. To date, these books have sold half a billion copies.

Mark's "lived-it" experience has shown him that people don't just want inspirational stories, they desperately crave them. Mark's life has revolved around sharing these kinds of stories.

How does this relate to you?

Here's where we go into how you can create your own redemptive story. If you're like everyone I've ever met, you've had catastrophically bad things happen to you. I can't reach out from these pages and talk with you about them. I wish I could spend time with you and get to know you and hear your story, but I can't.

What I can be certain of is, you've been through some rough times. I've heard stories of incest, drug abuse, schizophrenia, depression, kidney failure, blindness, financial catastrophe, a horrible divorce, surviving sex-trafficking, the death of a child . . . the ways life can be painful are, alas, virtually limitless.

How do you cope?

Write your story. In fact, write your autobiography—it can be very cathartic. Even better, rewrite your story, inviting in the parts that made you what you are today and will help you along the way to being all you yearn to be.

28. Stories Can Change Your Life

As you write about the bad parts; first, be totally honest. But second, wring every bit of knowledge and understanding and wisdom that you can from the anguishing experiences. What would you tell those who come after you about what it took to come through it?

Mark's own story of bankruptcy and a failed marriage were personally and desperately painful for him. And yet the way he frames both stories is that, although he failed, he wasn't a failure. Real failure only happens if you quit on yourself. There is always new possibilities looming in our future.

He learned to be more careful financially, and while he made mistakes in his first marriage, he's learned from them and he expects never to repeat them. He also frames pretty much every failure as an opportunity to be more empathetic and more understanding. He frames his failures as learning opportunities that propel him toward greater success.

What you just read in the last few paragraphs is about dealing with the seriously difficult events or circumstances in your life. Let's shift focus, pan away from those and focus now on the good parts of your life.

What went well? What are you proud of? Are there relationships that give you joy? In your story, celebrate them! Figure out how you can build on them and become more and more the person you want to be.

Of course, don't ignore the disastrous parts; they're a part of your life, and you own them. However, they don't own you. Your biography is the place to frame these events in the context of your entire life. They're only a part of your life, and it's unfair to judge your whole life by the worst days.

As Mark puts it, "These stories help us know our weaknesses so that we can grow and learn to become a better version of ourselves. The journey of the dramas, the trials, the tribulations, the joys, the breakthroughs, and the setbacks and all come together to sculpt who we are. Getting in touch with your own story is one of the most important things you will ever do," says Mark.

He summarizes why it's important to write your autobiography. "We need one another's stories, and that's why I created my new company, the Mark Victor Hansen Library. We are telling stories and having soul conversations."

But what if you're not a writer? What if you see the advantages of writing your autobiography but the thought of starting it and getting it done feels about as easy for you as climbing Mount Everest on crutches—without oxygen?

Mark's got you covered. Skip to the Epilogue.

> *You invent yourself. Be the C.I.O. of your life and future as the Chief Imagination Officer.*
> Mark Victor Hansen

Learn from Mark:

- In shaping your lives, there's almost nothing more important than the stories you tell yourself. We literally invent ourselves and we can keep re-inventing ourselves day-by-day for our entire lifetime.
- You can edit and change your story. When Mark's internal story was, "I'm a failure," he was despondent, disconsolate, and depressed. He could barely function When he reframed his story to, "My destiny is to be a speaker and writer to

28. Stories Can Change Your Life

help people," he became blessed with the energy to achieve unprecedented success.

- You have almost certainly had disasters in your life. Copy others who have reframed their stories so that the disasters led to growth and understanding, putting them on the path to becoming a better version of themselves.
- Getting in touch with your own story is one of the most important and impactful things you will ever do.

29 The Next Chapter

Mark was born thinking big. He's always been doing something larger than life.

- At nine years old, he sold more greeting cards than any young person and earned the equivalent of more than $12,500 in today's dollars. He wanted the seemingly impossible, an English racing bike. He figured out how to get it, and then he did what it took to earn the money to buy it.
- At sixteen, he wanted to create a band called the Messengers. With no musical experience and no experience in promotion, he was able to create the band, which at times would earn more money in an evening than his father earned in a year.
- In his twenties he was told that the odds of being able to earn a living by speaking were one in a thousand. He made the effort to learn how to do it. In short order Mark was giving four talks a day, and while still in his twenties, he was selling his talks for as much as $5,000 each.
- In his thirties he was perfecting his craft as a speaker. Very few speakers in the world were able to earn the $10,000 fees that he regularly earned.

29. The Next Chapter

- In his forties, after being turned down 144 times, he and Jack Canfield found a publisher for *Chicken Soup* for the Soul, and after an unpromising start, created a record-breaking bestseller.
- In his fifties, he was widely known as the #1 motivational speaker in the country. He was getting paid $35,000 a talk in this country. In China, he was regularly making $225,000 for three speeches.
- In his sixties, he made a list of 267 qualities, values, virtues, and characteristics that he was looking for in a wife and, incredibly, found them all in the soon-to-be Mrs. Crystal Dwyer Hansen.

> *"Big goals get big results. No goals gets no results or somebody else's results."*
> Mark Victor Hansen

What about his seventies?

Mark's pattern is to think big. After all, he's the one wrote *How To Think Bigger Than You Ever Thought You Could Think*. An important aspect is that in each decade of life he's moved on to bigger, more impactful activities. What is he doing now in his seventies?

Mark has in mind a major role for you in this enterprise. It's one that can make possible a fuller and more exciting life. Read more about the newest chapter, in the epilogue—The Mark Victor Hansen Library.

29. The Next Chapter

> *The best book ever written hasn't been written,*
> *because YOU haven't written it—yet!*
> Mark Victor Hansen

Learn from Mark:

- Read! With reading you get the lifetime of distilled wisdom from some of the world's greatest thinkers, doers, and contributors. Reading is a shortcut to success. It enables you to think bigger than you've ever thought.

- You can follow the example of the most successful and most innovative people. The following heroes are all readers: Andrew Carnegie, Warren Buffett, John Pitre, Michael Angelo, and Mother Teresa. And then there's Elon Musk, who says: "I was raised on books, and then, by my parents!"

- Books provide you with an ever-better future. Books enable you to translate good thinking into reaching your best potential.

- Books help secure your freedom. If you ever wonder about how important books are to a freedom, a culture, and civilization, just note that the first thing that all despots, tyrants, socialists, and communists like Hitler, Mussolini, Mao, and Stalin did was burn the books.

- Drink in the wisdom of the ages and then expand it. Follow Mark's example. He reads widely and then writes in such a way that he expands the wisdom. In his case, he's already either author or co-author of 318 books actively in print and being sold. He has 50,000 books in his library.

30 Conclusion

Many decades ago, I experienced a clear case of "runner's high," a sense of euphoria or extreme delight that can come when you've been running. I had been running longer and harder than usual, and suddenly the world around me seemed to radiate greater beauty than I ever imagined. The yellow buttercups in the field I was racing by seemed to glow like the Holy Grail. In the middle of this luminescent beauty, I heard a deep awesome voice querying me, "Mitzi, would you like to know the nature of good, and evil?"

"Yes!" I gasped.

The voice enunciated the following words, almost as if it were God Himself who was speaking, "Good is that which is energized by the healing and growth and enlightenment of others. Evil is that which seeks the pain, suffering, and stunting of others."

It occurs to me, as my journey with you comes to its end, that maybe the definition of what is good is the most useful measuring stick for evaluating Mark. Does he encourage healing, growth, and enlightenment?

It's clear that he's not perfect. He makes mistakes. He exaggerates. He can be, and for that matter, often is, unrealistic. He's gone bankrupt. He failed badly at his first

30. Conclusion

marriage. He's probably in court too often. He's made investments that turned sour. Even so, Mark's work has had unprecedented reach, encouraging uncountable numbers of people to transcend their limitations and to become more than they otherwise would have been.

At the beginning of our journey together in this book, I posed the question: Is Mark a real-life version of Howard Hill, the shady promoter from The Music Man? Or is he St. Mark, someone who is unrealistically good, an unworldly presence?

The answer is that Mark is neither. He's a real person, and he's not someone who bats a thousand. He makes mistakes and has had a collection of failures. But what he learned from those failures propelled him to ever greater successes. In the process, he's been a mentor and an inspiration to millions. He's a beacon for healing, growth, and enlightenment.

He's a larger-than-life force for good in a deeply troubled world.

I have had the privilege of living a hundred lifetimes in one lifetime. I want to inspire others to live more fully, wonderfully, and completely with this book.
Mark Victor Hansen

Epilogue

As we've already learned, Mark is not one to let grass grow under his feet. In January of 2022, he launched the Mark Victor Hansen Library. With his passion for the written word, Mark wants to encourage anyone who has the desire to publish a book.

If you have never considered publishing a book under your name, please consider the benefits. Authorship is a coveted credential and elevates the author in the eyes of friends, family, colleagues, and business associates. It's a wonderful way to promote yourself, your ideas and your philosophy for life.

MVH Library uses its global reach to provide clients with a superior experience for ghostwriting and publishing. We begin with a story strategy session to find the best story for you. It may be your biography or a nonfiction work featuring your business message. Or it may be a carefully crafted novel which captures the essence of who you are, what you believe, and what message you want to put out into the world. All our novels are inspired by the client and have the potential to reach the widest audience of readers.

We are proud to bring a talented team of ghostwriters who can write for almost every genre. This ranges from literary

Epilogue

fiction to mystery to senior adult. Let your imagination run wild and we'll work with you to bring it to life.

We will guide you through the whole process from conception through writing, editing, and ultimately publication.

Today is the day to take that first step.

Contact Us using the convenient tool on our website https://markvictorhansenlibrary.com and someone will be in touch soon.

We hope you will be part of this exciting journey with Mark, and you will allow us to publish your new book!

Please check the MarkVictorHansenLibrary.com for a lineup of current and upcoming titles.

We tell stories that are moving, emotional and instructive in all of your favorite genres:

- Literary Fiction • Women's Fiction • Family Saga
- Romance • Adventure • Mystery/Crime
- Suspense/Thriller • Science Fiction • Fantasy
- Horror/Paranormal
- Children's Books • Young Adult • New Adult
- Senior Adult • Humor/Comedy
- Screenplay • TV/Movie Treatment
- Narrative Non-Fiction • Historical Fiction • Biography

One final thought, in case you were wondering. I researched and wrote every word of this book, and for that matter, writing it was my idea. Although the MVHL has a team of talented ghost writers, this book wasn't written by one of them.

In Closing

A few moments captured in the Mark Victor Hansen life and times of a serial philanthropist and writer.

Crystal and Mark with Joel Osteen

From left to right: Mark, Astronaut Alfred Worden, Apollo 15 Lunar Mission, Jack Roosa, U.S. Air Force Pilot flew F-16 Falcon on 80 combat missions, and his dad was Astronaut Stuart Roosa who flew Apollo 14, and Astronaut Walt Cunningham, Lunar Module Apollo 7 Lunar Mission.

In Closing

Mark receiving the Horatio Alger Award in the Supreme Court with classmate and friend, Tom Selleck

Maya Angelou, publicist Arielle Ford, Jack and Mark on Maya's PBS show

Mark and Crystal with Olivia Newton John and her husband John Easterling

RELENTLESS | 239

In Closing

Mark building a Habit for Humanity home with the founder Millard Fuller, actress Bo Derick, and Cynthia Kersey, author of *Unstoppable*

Mark in Wyland's art studio painting with him, after finishing
Chicken Soup for the Ocean Lovers Soul
https://www.wyland.com/the-artist/

In Closing

Mark and Richard Branson at his famous Necker Island home in the Caribbean

Mark and Jim Rohn, America's Business Philosophers, talking to an audience of 5,000

In Closing

Tony Robbins, Dr. Jerry Clum, and Mark ready to talk before thousands of Chiropractors on Long Island

(left)James Cameron after making the movie *The Titanic* invited Mark to dinner at his home in Malibu, CA (Right) Mark with Nora Roberts, author of *Hidden Riches*. They had *Chicken Soup for the Romantic Soul* on the side of fifty million Diet Coke cases for six months. Together, their respective books raised enough money to get 15,000 kids scholarships into Boys and Girls Clubs.

242 Mitzi Perdue

In Closing

Mark and Somers White, speaker, author, consultant, who served in the Korean War

Horatio Alger wrote 'rags to riches stories' that got America out of the depression of 1898. Mark was inspired to write with the goal to do the same for his world.

In Closing

Personal Activities

Mark climbing Machu Picchu to the Temple of the Sun built by Incas in 1450 AD

Mark proceeded to Summit Huayna Picchu visiting the Temple of the Moon in Peru, considered one of the seven wonders of the world

In Closing

Mark and Crystal at the Boulder Bolder with 120,000 walkers and runners

Mark and Crystal with grandkids Everett, grand twins Jensen and Maddie, Preston and Brooke

In Closing

About Mitzi Perdue

Mitzi Perdue has had a lifelong fascination with what it takes to lead the best life. She got to watch up close and personal how her father co-founded and was President of the Sheraton Hotel chain, and she also got to watch how her late husband, Frank Perdue, built his father-and-son chicken company into a company that today employees 21,000 people.

Both men had tremendous focus, they had a penchant for action, and they had wide-ranging interests which led them to see opportunities that others missed. They were also men who developed tremendous talent stacks, and when they needed to learn a new skill, they made the time and took the effort to learn the new skill.

In addition, they were also both to the core family men and they loved and served their communities.

When three years ago, Mitzi became friends with Mark Victor Hansen (famous for the *Chicken Soup for the Soul* series) and his wife Crystal, she wondered how many of the same success traits she had observed in her husband and father would be found in Mark. In this book, she draws on a lifetime of experience as a writer and as a student of what it takes to lead a full life to create a book that she hopes will encourage and inspire everyone who reads it.

Mitzi's professional career includes being a former rice grower, past presidency of the 40,000 member American

Agri-Women, and as a writer, in the 1990s, her nationally syndicated column, "The Environment and You," was the most widely syndicated environmental column in the US.

Mitzi's purpose in life is to encourage people to be all they can be. She believes that inspiration is the best gift one person can give another because inspiration provides people with energy and direction. She wrote Relentless with the goal of sharing Mark Victor Hansen's astonishingly wise tips for growth and happiness, tips that can help people live fuller, more satisfying lives.

Her latest book *Rich Widows of Savannah Valley* will be available in September.

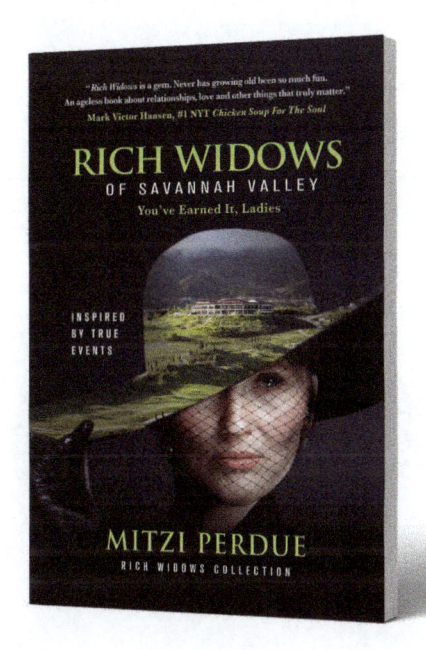